JO

C000075505

Discovering
Old Handwriting

SHIRE PUBLICATIONS LTD

Cover picture: Still life painted around 1675 (The Burrell Collection, Glasgow City Museums and Art Galleries). The scribe's equipment includes (from left to right) a wafer box, a stick of sealing wax, a pounce-shaker, a candle (for melting sealing wax – and to work by), an inkwell with pen holder, quill pen and seal matrix. The indenture in the foreground is written in a lawyer's engrossing hand on parchment with pendant seal. The mathematical treatise (back right) is titled in a humanistic script. The artist, 'Edward Collier Painter at London', signs his work (back left) in a copperplate round hand. The Latin tag, written in Roman capitals, wittily suggests that, just as the artist's hand improves upon nature (the painted picture seeming real), so the writer's hand works wonders. The creative writer lays bare the inner nature of man. Conversely he improves upon nature by concealing truth in a web of words or, through written forgery, gives reality to things which nature, and the hand of man, have neglected to create.

ACKNOWLEDGEMENTS
Illustrations are acknowledged as follows: by permission of the British Library, page 110; the Bodleian Library, Oxford, page 116; Norfolk County Council, pages 140-1; the Borthwick Institute of Historical Research, pages 142-3; by permission of The National Library of Wales, pages 144-5 and 157; the County Archivist of Durham and the Vicar of the Parish of Durham, St Oswald, pages 150-1; by permission of the Trustees of the National Library of Scotland, page 154; by permission of the General Assembly of the Church of Scotland, page 161. The line drawings are by Christine Clerk.

Published in 2001 by Shire Publications Ltd, Cromwell House, Church Street, Princes Risborough, Buckinghamshire HP27 9AA, UK. Website: www.shirebooks.co.uk
Copyright © 1995 by John Barrett and David Iredale. First published 1995; reprinted 2001. Number 285 in the Discovering series. ISBN 0 7478 0268 8.
John Barrett and David Iredale are hereby identified as the authors of this work in accordance with Section 77 of the Copyright, Designs and Patents Act 1988.

All rights reserved. No part of this publication may be reproduced or transmitted in any form or by any means, electronic or mechanical, including photocopy, recording, or any information storage and retrieval system, without permission in writing from the publishers.

British Library Cataloguing in Publication Data: Barrett, John. Discovering Old Handwriting. – (Discovering Series; No. 285). I. Title II. Iredale, David III. Series 652.109. ISBN 0-7478-0268-8.

Printed in Great Britain by CIT Printing Services Ltd, Press Buildings, Merlins Bridge, Haverfordwest, Pembrokeshire SA61 1XF.

Contents

1
Discovering Old Handwriting

Old handwriting is discovered every day in many different contexts. In the parish church, the worshipper is surrounded by texts on memorials and stained glass windows all lettered in quaint script – pleasing to the eye and intriguing to decipher. At home in the family Bible the principal events in the family history are lovingly inscribed in flowing script. Old wills and the title deeds to your own home, despite their crabbed and strange law hand, are readily readable – perhaps revealing something to your advantage!

Until the invention of printing in the fifteenth century writing was done with pen, pencil, brush or other tools held in the hand. This is **manuscript** writing, so known from the Latin words meaning 'handwriting'. A document written by hand is thus known as a manuscript. The handwriting in old manuscripts is studied by **calligraphers** (modern writers of artistic styles of handwriting) who adopt and adapt old alphabets to new graphic purposes. Old handwriting is studied by family and local historians as a preparation for research in parish registers, estate records and other **archives**. Handwriting may be a valuable clue to the personality of a long-dead writer – careful or slovenly, introvert or extravert. This is the art (or science) of **graphology**. Old handwriting is, of course, studied for its own sake, for the simple delight of discovering the wide variety and entrancing beauty of ancient writing styles.

The study of old handwriting is dignified with the proper name **palaeography** – from the Greek *palaios*, 'ancient', and *graphia*, 'writing'. The student of old handwriting is entitled to claim the pretentious designation of palaeographer.

2
Handwritings ancient and modern

The human species is distinguished by a passion for communication. The spoken word, supplemented by gesture, body posture and facial expression, served mankind well enough for tens of thousands of years. By word of mouth, knowledge was passed down the generations and information was communicated across continents. Seers and witch doctors developed phenomenal powers of memory. Poets and storytellers were entrusted with retelling, elaborating and passing on the history of the clan and tribe.

The beginning of writing represented a revolution in human development. Written communication added a new dimension to human culture and freed mankind from dependence upon mere memory. The use of pictures and abstract symbols to communicate a message, record a fact or tell a story was a dramatic development which can be traced back to the last ice age some 30,000 years ago. Stone-age hunters drew and painted pictures on the walls of deep caverns and other sacred places. The cave paintings in Spain and central France (dated to around 15,000 BC), showing animals of the hunt, communicate messages across the millennia, albeit in a language which we really cannot understand. The aborigines of Australia even today make paintings of animals and mystic symbols on sheets of bark, on everyday objects and on bare rock faces. These images tell stories of the Dreamtime, cast spells over people or beasts and communicate directly with the spirit world.

A picture serves as a graphic memory aid (**mnemonic**) to help

This cave painting at Lascaux in France vividly communicates the main elements of a stone-age legend: a bird-headed man, a bison wounded with spears, a bird.

the non-literate storyteller remember the sequence and main characters of a tale. The storyteller does not need even to speak the picture-writer's language to make some sense of the images. For example, a picture of a cow is comprehensible no matter what word the artist used to speak of the animal, whether the French word *vache*, Gaelic *bò*, Welsh *buwch*, English *cow* or some other word in a tongue long since forgotten. But a story told in pictures cannot begin to communicate every subtlety. Pictures alone cannot say whether 'the cow jumps over the moon' or 'the moon has gone under the cow'! Moreover, modern researchers who seek to read prehistoric picture-writings and do not belong to the writer's culture find it very hard to bridge the gap between prehistory and the present and to know what the image really means. Is the cow a character in a fable, a sort of hunting or fertility magic, a tally of the herdsman's stock, or an image of a goddess?

Mesopotamia

The story of writing (and of human civilisation) entered a dramatic new phase around ten thousand years ago. In Mesopotamia, in the Fertile Crescent of land watered by the rivers Tigris and Euphrates (modern Iran and Iraq), men first learned to plant crops and domesticate animals. Agriculture prospered as communities cooperated in sophisticated irrigation systems. Villages grew into towns, and towns into city-states ruled by powerful priests and kings. This complex civilised society demanded ever more accurate record-keeping. By means of stylised pictures (**pictographs**) scratched on to tablets of soft clay, the priest-kings of Mesopotamia kept account of the tribute brought to the temple (in livestock and produce). They kept tallies of enemies killed in battle, of slaves captured, bought and sold. As this first urban civilisation flourished, merchants and traders adopted the clay-tablet system for purchases or sales of cattle, timber, grain and so on, using simplified images of a cow, a man, a tree or an ear of barley – with scratched or impressed marks to denote quantities. This was being done by 3500 BC.

The action of scratching signs on to damp clay resembled, in miniature, the

A Mesopotamian clay-tablet pictograph of a goat. The dot above indicates the quantity '10'.

prehistoric ploughman scratching a furrow into the soil. The same word *skrabh* was used for both activities. This word passed into the major languages of Europe and Asia. It came into modern English in the forms *script, scribe, scrivener* and *scribble* via Latin and in the form *write* via German.

From around 3200 BC, for scribal convenience of grasping and writing on clay tablets, the whole pictograph system was rotated through ninety degrees anticlockwise so that each symbol now rested on its side. Symbols themselves were further simplified and stylised over the centuries and across the region.

From around 2500 BC the scribe's tools and formats were

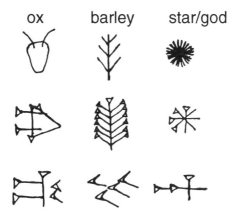

standardised in ways which remained little altered for over two thousand years. Scribes wrote on fist-sized, cushion-shaped, damp clay tablets. At the completion of writing, the tablets were usually just put out in the sun to dry naturally, though records for permanent preservation were baked hard. A special writing-stick (**stylus**) cut from a reed was adopted. This was cut in a variety of ways, perhaps with a triangular section at one end (for making letter-forms) and a round section at the other (for making number-marks). The cut of the stylus obviously affected the style of the writing. With the adoption of the wedge-shaped stylus, curves were eliminated and each pictograph was rendered in an economic handful of long-tailed wedge-shaped marks. Scholars have described this writing as **cuneiform**, meaning 'wedge-shaped'.

Most surviving cuneiform writings describe the day-to-day business of temple and municipal administration. A few narrate myths and legends, such as the deeds of the hero Gilgamesh or the account of the great flood sent by the gods to destroy mankind.

Using the round end of his stylus, the Mesopotamian scribe or accountant made complex arithmetical calculations. Cuneiform mathematics involved decimals and sexagesimals (sixties). Sexagesimal reckoning was preferred by *magi* (magicians, astronomers and astrologers). The sixties system survived to the modern world where we still have sixty seconds to a minute, sixty minutes to an hour, and 360 degrees in a full circle.

Mesopotamian scribes were the inventors of what palaeographers and printers now refer to as the **colophon** (from the Greek meaning 'finishing touch'). The scribe finished his document with his own name, the place of writing and the date of composition with, perhaps, also the title of the work. This information has continued to be required for all kinds of writing and may be crucial when studying a manuscript or printed book. In older printed books (from the fifteenth to the seventeenth century AD) the colophon was placed at the end of the text. From the seventeenth century onwards a **title page** at the beginning of the book superseded the colophon at the end.

Important cuneiform tablets were completely enclosed in a clay envelope. The name (but not the address) of the addressee was inscribed on the envelope. The document within was copied out on the envelope as a means of checking the original and as an aid against forgery – because unfired clay could easily be remoistened and the writing amended by unscrupulous scribes.

Witnesses to legal writings impressed their **seals** on to the soft clay of tablets and envelopes as a further means of authentication. The cylindrical seals were carved, in exquisite detail, from gemstone, bone or shell. Each bore a picture or cuneiform inscription unique to the owner (perhaps his name and titles), which the recipient of the document would immediately recognise. Seals, indeed, were in use before the development of writing. When marking a boundary, fixing the cover on a pot, tying up a parcel or closing ('sealing') a treasure vault or tomb, the owner pressed on a lump of clay to which he added his own personal seal. Access to the contents was difficult without breaking the clay seal.

The cuneiform pictograph system was expanded when scribes used their ordinary repertoire of signs to express an expanding dictionary of objects and ideas. Thus, the 'star' pictograph might in certain contexts convey the idea of 'god' or 'heaven'. Pictographs used to express ideas are known as **ideographs**, which basically means 'idea-writing'. The practice of employing the same symbol

This seal impression shows a Babylonian god watering a tree in a garden. The inscription is a late form of cuneiform.

to express a variety of ideas or words is known as **polyphony**, 'many sounds'.

The scribes next hit upon the revolutionary idea of using the pictograph of one word to represent other words or syllables similar in sound, just as if in written English a single pictograph represented both 'hair' and 'hare', 'key' and 'quay', 'sun' and 'son', 'tuber' and 'tuba', and so on. A symbol used in this way is known to palaeographers as a **phonogram** (that is, a 'sound-letter'). Mesopotamian scribes were, in effect, recognising that each individual sound or syllable in a language could be represented by its own individual symbol. And so the symbol representing the Sumerian word for a 'cow' , *ab*, could be used for the **ab** sound wherever it occurred in other words. Employing a variety of symbols to represent the same sound with different connotations is known as **homophony**, 'same sound'. This correlation of symbol to sound was a significant step forward to a simplified means of representing speech – the basis of written language today.

Cuneiform symbols were transferred from language to language across the Fertile Crescent. A symbol might be adopted into a new language either for its sound-value or for its simple meaning or for both! (This created a maze of challenges for future archaeologists, translators and palaeographers.)

In its developed form the cuneiform system was refined to some six hundred syllable symbols. Each symbol represented, basically, one consonant plus one vowel sound, for example, *ba, ca, da, fa* and so on, or one vowel plus one consonant as *ud, uf, ug*. Put simply, a vowel is a sound made by the vocal chords – a voiced sound (a e i o u). The Sumerians identified a e i u, four of the five vowels presently used in modern European languages. A consonant, on the other hand, is an unvoiced sound made in the mouth with the breath, tongue and lips (b c d f g h j th ch and so on).

Complex words were formed by a series of symbols. The name of the city of Nineveh required three syllable symbols of which the last syllable, in other contexts, could stand for the word *a*, meaning 'water'. To make his meaning plain the scribe prefixed confusable words with an unspoken **determinative** symbol indicating, say, 'city', 'animal', 'metal object' and so on. The determinative gave the reader advance warning of what sort of word to expect. As a further aid, a single cuneiform wedge was drawn to divide one word from another.

(city)   ni   nu   a
NINEVEH

Cuneiform signs were adapted to represent the syllables of various languages including Hittite, Akkadian, Hurrian, Elamite, Persian and Babylonian. The determinative sign (in brackets) was a reading aid only and was not spoken.

For over three thousand years the cuneiform system was refined and developed. It survived the rise and fall of the empires of Sumer, Nippur, Lagash, Ur of the Chaldees and Babylon. Cuneiform was used for fifteen major historical languages of the Fertile Crescent including Sumerian, Elamite, Assyrian, Eblaite and Hittite, the Akkadian tongue of Nebuchadnezzar's Babylon and the Persian of Darius and Xerxes.

After the decline of the ancient Persian empire cuneiform was lost to scholarship. Interest in cuneiform writing and the languages of Mesopotamia was revived in the eighteenth century AD as travellers and scholars explored the Middle East. Thousands of cuneiform clay tablets were unearthed by archaeologists digging down to the ancient temple archives which lay buried beneath the collapsed mud-brick cities on the plains of Iraq. Nearly every dwelling yielded one or two cuneiform documents, and the very bricks of the buildings bore cuneiform makers' marks and dedications to the gods. Cuneiform inscriptions are also known from inscriptions carved on to rock faces or chiselled across statues and tablets of stone (**stele**) proclaiming the deeds of rulers and the laws handed down by the gods.

The decipherment of cuneiform is one of the adventure stories of modern scholarship – and an object lesson for all palaeographers. The first task was to find the documents which might be buried (literally) in the ancient archives or offered for sale by shady dealers in the bazaar. Next, careful copies had to be made for the palaeographers to work from. Before the invention of photography, laborious **transcriptions** were prepared by hand, in ink on paper, by a scholar who might work in the comfort of a museum searchroom. More often, though, the scholar was obliged to make the transcription in less comfortable surroundings, perhaps perched atop a shaky ladder to read an inaccessible rock-face text or seated at a crude trestle under canvas to copy crumbling tablets just unearthed from an archaeological excavation. From a clear transcription the palaeographer next attempted a **transliteration** from the strange cuneiform symbols into the familiar alphabet. This process began with personal names which might be highlighted in some way in the original. Archaeologists and historians gave the palaeographer the name of the king or high priest in office at the time. Thus he might transliterate principal names. Next he might guess that repeated symbols or groups of symbols associated with personal names represented words and ideas such as 'king', 'great', 'god', 'lord' and so on. The discovery of dictionary tablets assisted transliteration. Texts written out in several different languages (especially where one version was a known language such as Old Persian) were particularly valuable aids to translators, who combined the skills of the linguist, the palaeographer and the codecracker to unravel the mystery of symbols used variously as phonograms, ideographs, syllables, determinatives and individual letters. The most famous scholar associated with this work was the soldier Henry Rawlinson, whose decipherment in 1846 of a cuneiform inscription of King Darius on the rock of Behistun in Persia was a landmark in the history of linguistics and palaeography.

From a transliterated text in which the meaning of certain words can be inferred, the palaeographer may begin to identify the language of the text (perhaps a tongue that nobody has spoken for thousands of years). With help from experts on the derivation of words a **translation** from the ancient language into a living tongue is at last possible.

Egypt
The writing of Egypt under the Pharaohs developed from a primitive pictograph system from around 3300 BC. Egyptian writing symbols are known as **hieroglyphs**, from Greek words meaning 'sacred carving', because writing was at first a priestly monopoly and was always a valued form of embellishment in temples

and tombs. About seven hundred symbols were in use during the Classical period (before 600 BC). For writing on stone the Egyptians (unlike their Mesopotamian contemporaries) did not simplify the forms of their writing symbols as they refined and added to the system. Egyptian writers cherished and preserved the realistic images of birds and animals which made up their writing system. Hieroglyphs in the traditional manner were still being inscribed on the buildings at Philae on the Nile in AD 394! The stylish beauty of the hieroglyphic symbols, which was so much appreciated by the carvers and tomb-painters of antiquity, charms the serious palaeographer and casual tourist alike even today.

The direction of Egyptian writing (right to left, or left to right, or vertically in columns) varied according to circumstances. The direction can be worked out even by the mere beginner because animal symbols were drawn facing the beginning of the line.

Though symbol-forms remained unreformed, the system progressed early from pictograph to ideograph. For example, the 'nose' symbol stood for the sense of 'smell' and the ideas of both 'joy' and 'contempt'.

Egyptian nose symbol.

The system next moved on to the **phonogram** stage in which the same written symbols are always used for the same sound, as in **phonetic** spelling. The hieroglyph for one word represented other words (or parts of words) which shared the same group of consonants, even though meaning something completely different. These hieroglyphs were phonograms only in terms of consonantal groups; vowel sounds were not written down in Egyptian script. There were three types of consonant grouping. The largest group of phonograms (around one hundred in number) represented just two consonants each. Thus the hieroglyph for a house stood for the consonants *pr* (the vowel-less version of the word for 'house'), and this symbol might represent sounds such as *par, per, pir, por, pur*. A second group (around fifty phonograms) stood for three-consonant sound-bites. The sacred scarab beetle sign stood for *hpr*; a bird sign for *tyw*. A very particular group of twenty-six phonograms stood for single consonants, such as the slug sign for *f*; flood-water for *n*; cup for *k*.

By putting together relevant sound-bites of one, two or three consonants, a whole vocabulary of words of several syllables could be built up, all without vowels but with determinatives as necessary to assist the reader.

For most purposes, the nature of the ancient Egyptian language, the context and the scribe's skill meant that vowel signs were not required. There were exceptions though. The Pharaoh's name was inscribed with a full panoply of vowels and consonants when painted or carved in the secret environs of the tomb or on the public façade of the temple. The name was protected against hostile magic within a charmed frame (notionally a circle of rope) known as a **cartouche**.

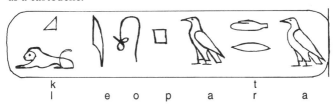

k
l   e   o   p   a   t   a
                                  r

In the development of Egyptian writing each new stage supplemented rather than replaced the one which went before. In a line of hieroglyphic script a symbol might stand for the object actually drawn, or for some idea associated conventionally with the object, or, phonetically, for just one sound-bite or even for a single letter in a word laboriously spelled out. Though probably no problem for the Egyptian reader, this presented considerable challenges for the palaeographers and historians of later ages.

The 'scribe' hieroglyph was formed of the scribe's equipment: a bag containing pigment, a palette for mixing the ink, a slender case to hold a selection of reed pens.

In addition to stately inscriptions on stone, the Egyptians also wrote in ink with a reed brush or pen on **papyrus** (a form of paper made from the papyrus reed which flourished on the banks of the Nile). For writing on papyrus a new style of script was developed, a relaxed hieroglyphic of symbols that might be more readily drawn in ink. This is known as **hieratic** writing, meaning 'sacred' because it was chiefly used by priests for religious purposes. Hieratic may be described in the jargon of palaeography as a **book hand**, that is a type of writing suitable for the copying of formal texts for maximum visual effect and legibility. Book hands recur in most later western scripts as examples of the 'best writing' of the time.

From hieratic yet a third style of writing was developed for use by businessmen and by the busy civil servants who administered the Pharaoh's estates and gathered the taxes. It was known as **demotic** – 'everyman's' script – and developed into an easy to use **cursive** style (from the Latin 'to run'), that is, with simple rounded sloped characters capable of being swiftly written for everyday use. Thus, at least three thousand years ago, three basic writing styles had been established for three particular purposes.

Exactly what all this writing meant was not understood until the finding near the town of Rashid (ancient Rosetta) in July 1799, by a party of Napoleon's soldiers, of an inscribed stone which listed the honours bestowed on the Pharaoh Ptolemy V Epiphanes (205-180 BC), who reigned after the Greeks conquered Egypt. At the top the characters were hieroglyphic, in the middle demotic, and at the bottom Greek. The stone, ceded to the British in 1801, was placed in the British Museum. Twenty years later, by comparing the hieroglyphic and demotic texts with the Greek, the Rosetta stone was deciphered, the code finally being cracked by a French scholar, Jean-François Champollion.

Asia, America and Northern Europe

Beyond the Middle East other inventive ancient civilisations devised symbolic communications systems. The Chinese developed a pictographic system before 2000 BC. The earliest Chinese symbols underwent a process of reshaping, though the essentials of the writing system were unaltered. Chinese writing remained, basically, a word-script (or idea-script) in which each word or concept was represented by a unique symbol. This system involved some fifty thousand symbols, though a basic set of perhaps four thousand symbols suffices for most day-to-day purposes. Chinese writing, unwieldy to western minds, was a principal instrument in the development and administration of a sophisticated society. The system was exported to Japan under the Han dynasty (206 BC to AD 220) and flourished there despite fundamental differences between the Chinese and Japanese languages.

In the Americas native civilisations invented pictographic systems. The Mayans of Central America (500 BC to AD 1200) developed complex mathematics and a precise astronomical calendar as well as mnemonic or pictographic writing. Texts were inscribed on the stones of statues and temples and painted on deerskin or bark paper. The Mayan system was taken up by the Aztecs who rose to pre-eminence in Mexico during the fourteenth century AD and flourished until the Spanish conquest of the sixteenth century. The Central American system fell from use as native civilisations collapsed, so surviving texts cannot now be fully understood.

The Inca empire, stretching from Ecuador through Peru to Chile,

A fragment from an Aztec pictograph manuscript found at Ixcaquixtla, Mexico.

reached its zenith during the fifteenth century AD. Across the Inca empire complex messages were communicated and detailed administrative records maintained by means of the *quipu*. This was a bundle of knotted cords. Each cord conveyed a separate piece of information according to the colour and ply of the string and the position of the knot. *Quipu* accounts were kept during periods of up to twenty years, recording tribute paid by each district. Complex calculations were effected by means of pebble counters and coloured beans.

In northern France, Britain and Ireland from around 4500 BC cultural development took a different turn. Writing was not invented. Carvings made here were not representational. Realistic images of animals or objects may even have been taboo, so the first pictographic steps towards a writing system could not be taken. Instead, monuments and sacred places were inscribed with a limited range of symbols including circles, concentric rings, zigzags, axe-head shapes and (more rarely) spirals or linear patterns. Some of these are known as *cup-and-ring* marks. The carvings probably reflected and communicated the conceptual concerns of prehistoric priests and people. They may relate to the cycles of the seasons: the simple annual cycle of the sun and stars and the complex 18.61 year cycle of the moon, motions which governed everyday life and determined the siting and orientation of tombs and temples.

15

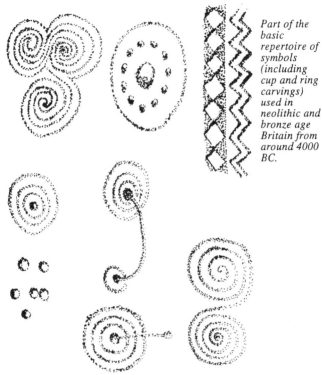

Part of the basic repertoire of symbols (including cup and ring carvings) used in neolithic and bronze age Britain from around 4000 BC.

Semitic scripts

Western Asiatic peoples are described as Semites because they are supposedly descended from Shem, son of Noah. The West Semitic peoples of Sinai and Palestine were in close contact with Egypt and indeed were from time to time within the Pharaoh's empire. Canaanites of Ugarit, Philistines (who gave their name to Palestine) and Hebrews all learned the value of reading and writing from the Egyptians. West Semitic scripts evolved around 1800-1300 BC. The Semitic peoples adopted just the single consonant element of the hieroglyphic system. They brought out of Egypt some thirty symbols.

The shape of these symbols derived from the hieroglyphic (hieratic) originals.

 Egyptian hieroglyph transformed into a Semitic symbol.

16

The names and sound-values of the symbols were strictly Semitic. Thus the 'house' hieroglyph (Egyptian **pr**) in a special form denoting a 'courtyard' was now named *betu* (West Semitic word for 'house') and stood for the *b* sound in the Semitic language; the 'water' hieroglyph (Egyptian **nwy**) was renamed *mayyuma* (West Semitic for 'water') and stood for the consonant *m*. The sound-value of each letter was that of the first letter of its name: thus *d* is the letter *daleth*, *z* is *zayin*, and so on.

house   water

This writing system was eagerly seized upon by the Phoenicians who occupied a strip of coast now in Syria. From the ports of the twin cities of Tyre and Sidon Phoenician merchants established a trading empire which extended from the shores of Britain to the gates of India. It was vital for this trading people to keep accurate records and to communicate in a practical form of writing. Before 1100 BC Phoenician scribes had reduced the number of letters required to just twenty-two. Their script was written from right to left. This direction of writing thereafter governed the writing conventions of other cultures, including Arabic and Hebrew.

Over many centuries the basic script (still a consonant-set without need for vowels) was further refined. Letter-forms were altered to suit the tastes of different tribes and peoples. A notable change was the rotation of letter-forms. For example, the basic Phoenician letter *shin* W was turned through ninety degrees by the South Semitic tribes.

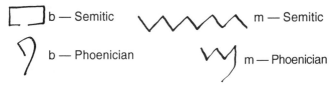

Symbols for the b-sound and m-sound simplified by the Phoenicians.

Phoenician 'shin' turned through 90 degrees by the South Semites.

Semitic writing was adopted and adapted by various western Asiatic peoples in Turkey, Syria, Arabia and Cyprus; in Punic

17

(Phoenician) colonies across the Mediterranean; and by the inhabitants of Moab, Canaan and Israel (the Hebrews).

A South Arabian (South Semitic) script may have derived from the Canaanite before 1300 BC. This was in turn exported to neighbouring nations, including Ethiopia, before 1000 BC. Scribes in Ethiopia added marks to consonant symbols to indicate the vowel which followed. South Semitic is also significant in developing angular letter-forms which supplied the basis for Greek writing.

The Aramaic tribes (of Syria and northern Iraq) developed a script which eventually indicated both consonant sounds and vowel sounds, though vowels were assigned certain consonant symbols (just as in English writing **y** may work as a consonant in y**et** but as a vowel in fl**y**). Aramaic writing was exported (through conquest and deportation) into Assyria during the eighth century BC, and extended its influence as far afield as India.

Aramaic script was employed for writings of all kinds in Palestine, most notably for religious texts. The most famous of these are the *Dead Sea Scrolls*, inscribed by communities of religious Jews of the radical monastic Essene sect. Aramaic is the language of the earliest surviving written texts of the Bible. Jewish scholars claimed that Aramaic script was invented by the prophet Ezra. It was considered a holier hand than Hebrew and so became the standard book hand of orthodox Jews throughout the middle ages. Genuine Hebrew writing was preserved, fortunately, as the usual script of the Samaritans (the despised neighbours of the Jews).

Syriac (Syrian) Aramaic was devised in the region of Edessa in Mesopotamia, a district which was to become a power base for early Christianity. The script was used by early Christian missionaries to the Semites from around 150 AD. Examples of the script have been found as far away as China and the script continues in use today among Syrian Christians worldwide.

From the Nabatean Aramaic script of the Roman period emerged the Arabic script of the sixth century – though Arabic dialects had been spreading across Arabia and Palestine since the first century. Manuscripts in Arabic script were widely disseminated as Islam became a dominant faith from Spain in the west to Indonesia in the east. Arabic scribes were instrumental in preserving, communicating and developing the accumulated wisdom of the Mediterranean world following the decline of the Roman Empire, in the fields of literature, philosophy, astronomy, alchemy, mathematics and medicine.

Greece

From around 3200 BC agricultural communities of the Aegean

islands and mainland were transformed. Their economy was revolutionised through contacts with Egypt and the Middle East. Metal implements and weapons were introduced. Pictorial seals were stamped on to damp clay as a means of security for property. Merchants learned the advantages of written communication, perhaps from Mesopotamia or Anatolia (Turkey). Initially the writing was pictographic or ideographic but bureaucrats in thriving towns and citadels successfully devised an Aegean set of syllabic symbols to satisfy the ordinary local demands of government and commerce. The text was usually written in lines across a clay tablet using a stylus, thought it is probable that pen, ink and papyrus were just as commonly employed. One script, known to archaeologists as **Linear A** and dating from before 1650 BC, was written from left to right, possibly in a non-Greek language. This has not been satisfactorily deciphered.

Another script of the period 1500-1150 BC, known as **Linear B**, recorded an early form of Greek spoken at the administrative centre of Knossos on the island of Crete. The pictorial symbols were highly stylised to indicate some ninety open syllables (that is, syllables ending in a vowel). Linear B (which had no convenient bilingual translation or names of famous kings) was deciphered by Alice Kober and Michael Ventris between 1943 and 1953.

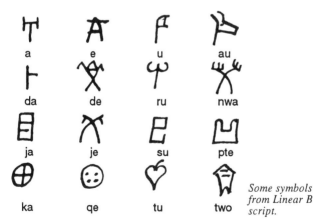

Some symbols from Linear B script.

Most surviving documents contain inventories of goods at the palaces of Minoan kings (rulers of Crete until about 1380 BC). The successor Mycenaean civilisation on the mainland and in Crete is also recorded until its disintegration around 1200 BC. It is this Minoan-Mycenaean culture of the Aegean region during the bronze age that the Greek poet Homer depicted centuries later. Probably Homer based his epics of the *Odyssey* and *Iliad* on songs and stories transmitted by word of mouth, but he may have acquired knowledge through written record. Minoan-Mycenaean script was lost as a medium of communication by around 1150 BC.

A completely different writing system – essentially the Phoenician system – was acquired by the Greeks around 900 BC, probably through trading contacts with Phoenicia. From this Phoenician connection the Greeks at first learned to write from right to left in lines across the page. For a relatively brief period the lines of Greek writing ran alternately left to right and right to left. This is described by the Greek term **boustrophedon**, literally 'following the ox-furrow', because the Greek ploughman worked in this manner, walking to and fro across his field behind his team of oxen. Eventually the familiar western left to right line of writing predominated. Perhaps as a result of these sharp changes of writing fashion, various letter-forms became reversed as mirror images while others turned through ninety degrees.

Greek letters reversed.

The Greeks adopted the Phoenician, Hebrew and Aramaic names for their letters and, for the most part, also Phoenician sound-values. Thus, for example, Phoenician **beth** was called *beta* by the Greeks and used for the *b* consonant, Hebrew **taw** became *tau* (t); Aramaic **lamed** became *lambda*.

Certain Phoenician letter-forms, representing consonantal sounds not used in Greek dialects, were ultimately pressed into service as Greek vowels. The table shows how the names and the basic shapes of these letters survived, and how their sound-values changed. The sounds include such familiar and unfamiliar vocal tricks as the glottal stop, made by the sudden opening and closing of the windpipe – heard in Cockney English in 'butter' pronounced 'bu'er', and the guttural sound, produced in the back of the throat, heard in the Scots **ch**, as in loch.

Writing down vowels was a significant step in the development of writing.

The Greeks adopted a standard order for arranging their twenty-four letters, beginning with *alpha* and *beta*, hence our word 'alphabet'. This Greek alphabet was, in the jargon of palaeographers, a **majuscule** script made up of large letters of equal height. The third letter was pronounced as hard **g**, which the Phoenician name (*gimel*) and Greek name (*gamma*) both suggest. The tenth letter

PHOENICIAN (consonant)			GREEK (vowel)		
Name	**sound**	**shape**	**Name**	**sound of letter**	**shape**
aleph	glottal stop		*alpha*	**a**	
he	**h**		*epsilon*	short **e**	
cheth	roughly breathed **h**		*eta*	long **e**	
yod	**y**		*iota*	**i**	
'ayin	guttural		*omikron*	short **o**	
'ayin	guttural		*omega*	long **o**	
vau	**v**		*upsilon*	**u**	

stood for the **k** sound (or hard **c**).

The Greek alphabet proved to be a marvellous instrument for facilitating commercial transactions among the scattered cities and islands of the Aegean. For particular purposes, especially for speedy writing by merchants and administrators, the stately majuscule letter-forms were adapted to new cursive shapes characterised by small-sized letters sprouting **ascenders** (for example, *delta*) and dropping **descenders** (for example, *zeta*). Individual letters were rounded and perhaps sloped when written quickly, even joined together by attaching strokes known as **ligatures**. Thus the script could be described as **current** (from the Latin word meaning 'to run') or joined-up handwriting. The Greeks, inventors of so much else that is now taken for granted, were thus the originators in Europe of the first joined-up small-letter writing. To palaeographers this type of script is known as **minuscule**. This minuscule script was developed by the second century BC and continued in use throughout the next Roman period. Modern mathematicians and scientists still use such Greek small letters such as *pi* and *mu*.

Aα alpha	Bβ beta	Iγ gamma	Δδ delta	Ⱶε epsilon	Zʒ zeta
Hη eta	Θϑ theta	Iι iota	Kκ kappa	Ⲣλ lamda	Mμ mu
Nν nu	Ξξ xi	Oο omikron	Πϰ pi	Pρ rho	Σσ sigma
Tτ tau	Yυ upsilon	Φφ phi	Xχ chi	Ψψ psi	Ωω omega

The Greek alphabet in majuscule and minuscule forms, showing the name of each letter.

Greek was spoken by many early Christians. Greek was the language of St Paul's epistles (letters) to the Corinthians, Ephesians and Philippians. Early Christians adopted as a sacred sign a **monogram** (a single symbol) combining the two Greek letters *chi* and *rho*. These were the first two letters of the Greek word *Khristos* ('Christ') meaning 'anointed one'. The cross shape of the letter *chi* was doubly symbolic in terms of Jesus' death. Ultimately, though, the ancestry of the letter may be traced back to an Egyptian 'fish' hieroglyph and also to a Mesopotamian 'fish' pictograph. The sign of the fish was also the symbol most used by the early Christians.

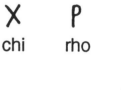

Greek script was adopted widely across the classical world, through the influence of Greek merchants and colonists. The Etruscans of Tuscany (in Italy) used the script from before 800 BC, adapting letter-forms to their own taste and tongue.

Rome

The alphabet was taken up by the Latin-speaking people of the Rome district (Latium), probably during the seventh century BC.

As subjects of Etruscan overlords, the Romans learned their letters in the rounded Etruscan (rather than the angular Greek) form. Thus Roman *C D P S* were curvaceous compared with Greek forms. Roman *C* was pronounced hard (**k**). For the hard Roman **g** a modified *C* was devised which, by adding a cross-stroke, became *G*. The letter-form *K* was scarcely used beyond the Greek word *Kalendae* (name for the first day of the Roman month). This could also be spelled *Calendae* (and often was in medieval Latin writing).

The Roman letter H

| West Semitic | Phoenician | early Greek | later Greek |

Latin speakers often dropped their aitches. Roman *H* derived from West Semitic *hotu* 'fence', revolved in Phoenician and simplified in Greek.

Greek *lamda* was gently revolved to become Roman *L*. Greek *rho* (sounded as **r**) was given an extra stroke to become Roman *R* ; unaltered it served as Roman *P* (sounded as **p**). Curvaceous *Q*, discarded by the Greeks, was revived to serve for the important **qu** sound in Latin. *Chi* was taken into Latin as *X* for the Latin sound **ks**; *xi* was not adopted. *Upsilon* was adapted for the Latin **u** (both short and long): the shape was modified into rounded *U* and angular *V*. The two forms were used interchangeably by Roman (and medieval) scribes as both vowel **u** and consonant **v**, for example in the word *UIRVS*, normally *VIRUS*, meaning 'poisonous slime'. Roman scribes did, however, encourage the use of *V* as consonant and *U* as vowel, though for monumental work such as carved inscriptions *V* was preferred, even as a vowel.

Latin writers dropped the Greek symbols for *th ks kh ph ps*. For *f* (for example, in *filia*, daughter), Roman scribes added a stroke to Greek *gamma* to create Roman *F*. The convenient *F* letter infected even words which derived from the Greek and should have been spelled with a *Ph*, a trend which continued in modern European writing, for example with the spelling 'fantasy' which should, properly, be 'phantasy'.

Ten Greek letters were taken up by the Romans with little or no alteration in shape: *A B E I K M N O T Z*. The *I* served as both vowel **i** and consonant **j**, pronounced in Latin as English **y** as in 'yet').

The classical Latin alphabet thus consisted of twenty-three letters arranged: *A B C D E F G H I K L M N O P Q R S T V X Y Z*, to which the Romans gave native names. These names underlie the names used (with local variations) across western Europe. The English names for the letters – 'bee, cee, dee, eff, el, em, en' and so on – are thus ultimately of Roman origin.

Egyptian hieroglyph	West Semitic (Sinai/Canaan)	Phoenician	Greek	Latin
'ox'	alpu 'ox'	aleph	alpha	A
'house'	betu 'house'	beth	beta	B
'water'	mayyuma 'water'	mem	mu	M
'snake'	nahashu 'snake'	nun	nu	N
'eye'	aynu 'eye'	ayin	omicron	O
'mouth'	pe 'mouth'	pe	pi	P
'head'	rashu 'head'	resh	rho	R
'mountain/ desert'	shin 'land'	shin	sigma	S

The development of key letters of the alphabet from 3000 BC to Roman times.

Roman writing in Britain and Ireland

The Latin alphabet was introduced to the Celtic peoples of Britain and Ireland as European merchants travelled the islands in pursuit of business. Celts were aware of majestic Roman lettering long before Julius Caesar invaded with his legions. Native coins circulated widely in the course of trade. These bore tribal or royal symbols as well as the ruler's name in more or less dignified Roman letters. British palaeographers refer to these large letters as 'square capitals' or 'monumental capitals': square because they are strictly geometrical and, in theory, each letter fits a square (or half-square) box; capital (from Latin *caput,* head) because they were carved on important monuments and appeared at the head or beginning of chapters, sentences and important words.

This was a majuscule script with letters of equal height, though

Formal capitals for the inscription on a Roman legionary's tombstone at Gloucester.
RUFUS SITA EQUES C[O]HO[RTIS] VI
TRACUM ANN[ORUM] XL
STIP[ENDIORUM] XXII
HEREDES EXS TEST[AMENTO]
F[ACIENDUM] CURAVE[RUNT]
H[IC] S[ITUS] E[ST]

Rufus Sita, trooper of the 6th cohort of Thracians aged 40; of 22 years service, lies buried here; his heirs had this erected according to the terms of his will

Q trailed a tail below the line of writing as the exception. In the most elegant versions, a small cross-stroke was added at the head or tail of the vertical stroke of a letter. This is known as a **serif**. The script was adopted from the first century AD throughout Britain. Merchants and religious missionaries were probably the agents in introducing writing to Ireland.

Writing in monumental capitals was a slow business so there evolved a freer hand for everyday use. This was still a script of capital letters but very much simplified, condensed and excellent for writing in ink on papyrus or parchment. The letters are known as **rustic capitals**, perhaps because of their rustic simplicity. The tall narrow letters show pronounced thick and thin strokes with heavy square or wavy serifs. *I* and *L* were very similar. *F* raised its head above the line to differentiate from *E*. The base angle of *V* became curved while *A* lost its crossbar.

In practice, rustic lettering was employed as the formal book hand of the Roman empire – a best writing for published books copied by professional scribes, whose output on scrolls of parchment or papyrus included the works of Roman poets such as Horace and

25

Cursive script on a lead plaque: a curse nailed to the front door of a citizen of Roman Londinium.
T[ITUS] EGNATIUS TYRAN[N]US DEFICTUS EST ET P[UBLIUS] CICEREIUS FELIX

Titus Egnatius Tyrannus is cursed and Publius Cicereius Felix too.

Virgil, of historians such as Tacitus and Julius Caesar, the Greek classics, and the books of the Bible and the Church Fathers.

But even rustic capitals were not sufficiently business-like for the day-to-day written communications of an expanding empire. Before the first century AD scribes followed the Greek example and developed a cursive, and ultimately even a current, handwriting. The script had economical, sloped letter-forms based on rustic capitals: letters could even be joined by ligatures to increase speed. The script was, in effect, minuscule, that is, with ascenders and descenders from the main line of writing and well suited to writing in ink on papyrus or on wax memorandum tablets. In Britain soldiers economically wrote on wafer-thin slats of wood. Graffiti on walls is usually in a very cursive script! Roman cursive letter-forms are the ancestors of the small-letter writing we use today.

Λ	B	C	D	E	F
λ	λ	Ξ	δ	ε	ℱ
α	℔	ι	d	ε	ρ
G	H	I	K	L	M
Ϲ	ㅓ	ι	k	⌐	M
ʒ	h	ι	ʞ	ℓ	m
N	O	P	Q	R	
μ	δ	ϲ	Q	ϒ	
n	o	ρ	ϥ	ℾ	
S	T	V	X	Y	Z
ʃ	⊤	v	✗	Υ	z
ϒ	ϲ	u	⋋	Υ	ℤ

Table showing how Roman rustic capitals were developed into small letters for use in everyday written communications.

26

Ogham

Ogham script (named after Ogmios, Celtic god of eloquence) developed for monumental inscription in Ireland from the second century AD and was exported thence in the baggage of Irish warlords and Christian evangelists to Pictland, Wales and Cornwall. Ogham characters encoded the vowels and consonants of the Roman alphabet as a series of horizontal or slanting strokes. These were typically carved on to the edges of memorial monoliths, Pictish symbol stones and Christian monuments marked with the sign of the cross.

The ogham alphabet

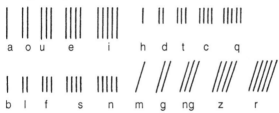

Ogham inscriptions generally include personal names, as for instance *CUNACENA*, carved on a slim flagstone from Coolmagart, County Kerry (now re-erected at Dunloe). These Celtic personal names were usually inscribed in the genitive case, as for instance *ICORIGAS*, 'of Icorix', at Brynkir, Gwynedd, meaning '[the stone] of Icorix'. Oghams include the characteristic Celtic *mac*, 'son of, kin of' (usually in the forms *maqq*, *meqq* or *maqi*) as in *MAGLICUNAS MAQI*

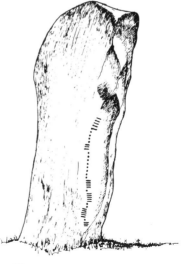

The Lang Stane of Auquhollie, Kincardineshire. The memorial to an Irishman dates from around AD 600. It reads from the bottom up FADH DONAN UI TEN... (here) sleeps Donan son of Ten...

27

CLUTARI, '[the stone] of Maglicu son of Clutarios', inscribed on a memorial stone at Nevern, Dyfed, and *EBICATOS MAQI MUCO*, on a memorial fashioned from a column found among the ruins of the Roman town of *Calleva* (Silchester, Hampshire). Sometimes such inscriptions recite a genealogy extending back several generations. Oghams carved on the Lang Stane of Auquhollie, Kincardineshire, include the Irish *ui* ('son of, descendant of'), an inscription which reads from bottom to top with vowels represented by dots rather than bars.

Runes

The alphabet idea captured Germanic imagination before the second century AD. The northern letters were known as **runes** – from a word implying mystery and magic. The runic alphabet (known as **futhork** from the sound values of its first six letters, *FUThORK*) comprised some twenty-four signs, adaptations from the Greek, Etruscan and Roman, and original coinings to represent peculiarities of barbarian speech. The stiff stick-shaped signs were conspicuously adapted to the needs of craftsmen working in stone, ivory, wood and metal.

The Anglo-Saxon futhork

f u th o r k g w h n i j ė p x
s s t b e m l ng oe d a ae y
ea ḡ k k̄

Runic lettering flourished until the eleventh century, most notably for monumental inscription and in magical contexts. A warrior's weapon gained secret power from runes chased, engraved or inlaid in gold and silver. For instance, a ninth-century Saxon knife (of a type known as a *scramasax*), found in the Thames at Battersea, bears the name of its owner (Beagnoth) together with a cabalistic (ritual) recitation of a twenty-eight letter futhork. On the eighth-century Anglian cross at Ruthwell, Dumfriesshire, the main inscription, carved up one side and down the other, is a runic rendering of the obscure Anglian poem *The Dream of the Rood*, a weird synthesis

b ea g n o th

of the Germanic myth of the pagan god Balder and the Christian passion of the rood (the Old English word for 'cross').

Runic memorial stone at Thornhill, Yorkshire, about AD 750.
+ Ea DRED
SETE AEFTE
EaTEENNE
+Eadred set up [this stone] for the lady Eateya

Runic inscription died out during the eleventh century but symbols which proved too useful to abandon were absorbed into the Anglo-Latin alphabet. *Wen* continued into the fourteenth century representing the English consonant **W** not supplied by the Latin alphabet. Thereafter *wen* rapidly lost ground to the various single and double forms of **U** and **V**. The *W* probably achieved single-letter status as early as 1100 though might be used interchangeably with *U* and *V* as late as the seventeenth century – an ambiguity whose echo is still heard through the name 'double U' for *W*.

Thorn, representing **th**, survived to the end of the fifteenth century, though increasingly rendered as *y*, which it resembled. In this form the letter became a usual feature of sixteenth-century writing, flourishing through the seventeenth century and surviving late in the eighteenth, most typically with the assistance of superscript letters, to give y^e for 'the', y^t for 'that', y^m for 'them', o^{yr}, for 'other'. This usage survives to this day in such contexts as Ye Olde Worlde Tea Shoppe.

Uncial and half-uncial scripts

Roman lettering was early adopted in place of Greek by the western Christian church for business and devotional documents. From the fourth to the eighth century sacred texts were written in an open, rounded, buxom book hand, written very large for maximum effect and known as **uncial**, 'inch-high', lettering.

Characteristic letter forms of uncial script.

λ B ᴆ ᴇ ꜰ hꞁ ꝳ p q ʀu

a B d e F h L m P q R U

Texts ran on without spaces between words. Abbreviation and punctuation were rare. Letters such as *B, N* and *R* retained capitular form but *a, e, m* substituted curves for classical angles. *V* softened

29

A co[m]pascha usque
pentecosten
*This phrase from a gospel
book written in English
uncial script of around AD
700 reads 'From the Passion
[Eastertide] until Pentecost
[Whitsuntide]'.*

into *U*, serving as both vowel and consonant; *d* sprouted a leftward
curving ascender; *F*, *P*, *q*, put down descenders; *h* and *L* raised
straight ascenders.

Under the influence of uncial script and Roman cursive a new
type of handwriting developed during the fourth century in Mediterranean Europe. Only partly uncial, or written just half the uncial
size, the script has come to be known in palaeography as **half-
uncial**. This was essentially a neat small minuscule script with
distinct ascenders and descenders, for example, to the letters *d f g h
p q*, and long *s*. Uncial *N* was retained, *g* could resemble the figure
5, while the letter *r* can be confused with *n*, and *t* with *c*. Mediter-

Characteristic letter-forms of half-uncial script.

a d f g h N p q r long t
s

ranean half-uncial influenced the development of national scripts
of the Goths, Vandals, Franks and other migrants into the territories of the former Roman empire. Scribes working in the monasteries of Christian Britain and Ireland were by no means isolated from
these changes. Half-uncial was adopted widely there, probably
during the fifth century, under the influence of Christian missionaries, men in the mould of St Palladius and St Patrick.

ҺΛBENTURExEꟼꟼDLΛRIΛ

*This half-uncial phrase reads (in Latin) 'habentur exemplaria' meaning
'an instance is considered'.*

Insular half-uncial

In Ireland scribes taught the half-uncial script. The earliest
example of the handwriting can be read on the Springmount Bog
tablets (now in the National Museum of Ireland) written about the
year 580. The *cathach*, 'battle-book', of St Columba, a collection

of psalms for carrying into battle as a talisman, is traditionally dated to the same era. The half-uncial of Ireland was employed across Britain, wherever Irish religious influence was strong, down to the ninth century. The script was different from the uncials of mainland Europe and thus is distinguished by palaeographers as the **insular** (or island) **half-uncial**. Irish Christians took the insular script to Northumbria, where, in the monastery of Lindisfarne, the Englishman Eadfrith and his colleagues in the writing-room evolved a distinctive and reformed insular half-uncial. It is seen at its best in the *Lindisfarne Gospels* of around the year 700 (now in the British Library).

This insular half-uncial script from a gospel book of around AD 700 reads (in Latin) 'incipit evangelium' meaning 'here beginneth the gospel'.

The insular script was exported to continental Europe by travelling Irish evangelists and through the traffic in precious manuscripts made as gifts for popes, princes and prelates. Insular script was voluptuously rounded. The *a* was closed and might sport rightward extensions at head and base; *e* was rounded and closed; flat-topped *g* dangled a curving tail; the diagonals of *N* dropped towards the foot of the letter, though some scribes preferred *n*; *r* was rounded, with a descender; tall *S* rose above the line; small flat-headed round-bottomed *t* predominated; *x* splayed curvaceously. Ascenders of *b h l* and descenders of *f p q* extruded

Characteristic letter-forms of insular half-uncial script.

stumpily. Letters were topped with jaunty leftward-flying pennants. For displayed matter (initial pages, headlines, etc) scribes affected jaggedly angular varieties of capitals and uncials. The script was widely employed by masons for memorial stones and crosses.

ÓAGIOS HALLhEUS

ÓAGIOS MATTHEUS

The angular display capitals were written around AD 700 in typical insular (British and Irish) script. 'Óagios' is the early medieval Greek word for 'saint'.

This memorial stone at Clonmacnois, County Offaly, of around AD 850 bears formal insular half-uncial lettering. The Irish inscription reads 'or do thuathal saer' meaning 'say a prayer for Toole the craftsman'.

The majority of early insular manuscripts now extant (perhaps the majority produced) are devotional texts: psalters, testaments and gospels. A book was far more than an information system; indeed the saints who knew their Bible by heart needed no written crib. Making a book was an act of devotion; the finished product an object, sacred in itself, for veneration. The careful transcription of text was a humbling self-discipline and, once written, the word was honoured – all but engulfed – by gorgeous ornament. Capitalised initials and frontispieces were overwhelmed in a welter of costly colour made from mineral substances such as yellow orpiment, green malachite, scarlet realgar and ultramarine lapis lazuli. Rounded letters mutated into fabulous shapes of man, beast and monster or sprouted into interwoven tendrils of plants. Artists enjoyed drawing the pagan Celtic *triskele*, a symbolic figure of three legs radiating from a common centre. The page of text became a canvas for individual invention. Most sumptuous of all perhaps were gospel books such as the *Codex Aureus* or Golden Book made at Canterbury around 750 (now in the Royal Library, Stockholm), its text inscribed in golden uncials on purple *vellum* (calf-skin).

Decorated lettering from the 'Book of Kells', about 800: 'dixerunt' meaning 'they have said'.

Spiky minuscule

At the close of the seventh century monastic scribes began to produce their documents in a cursive minuscule of a decidedly small and spiky nature. This was the script of Irish and Anglo-Saxon (English) monasteries. The Venerable Bede's *Ecclesiastical History of the English People* was copied out time and time again in spiky minuscule in the monasteries of Wearmouth and Jarrow where the author resided. The small neat script was much used by **glossators**, men who wrote word

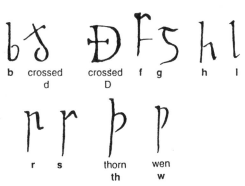

b	crossed d	crossed D	f	g	h	l

r	s	thorn th	wen w

Characteristic letter-forms of spiky minuscule.

33

for word translations (usually in English) between the lines of difficult Latin texts.

Characteristic of the insular spiky minuscule were the runes *thorn* and *wen*; the emphatic ascenders of *b h l* rising tall and finished with a leftward-facing triangular serif; *f r s* dropping pointed descenders. The descender of flat-topped *g* was rounded or looped (resembling a modern printed g). Crossed *D* and *d* represented *th*, surviving alongside *thorn* into the fifteenth century, by which time, however, an ordinary *d* was written, incidentally transforming the Old English word *morthre* into modern English 'murder'.

Spiky minuscule remained in use in England and Wales into the eleventh century, notably for English personal names and perambulations of land boundaries written in English (rather than Latin) in formal **diplomas** (see Glossary), writs and charters. Spiky minuscule was the hand of poets writing verse epics such as the legend of the hero Beowulf and witty riddles to demonstrate the writer's verbal virtuosity.

Cwico wæs ic ne cwæth icwiht

'Alive was I but did not speak'. A phrase from a riddle written in insular minuscule around the year 880.

A somewhat expanded angular species of insular minuscule was preferred until the seventeenth century for **glossing** (translating) and copying the classic texts of Ireland: *Annals of Inisfallen*, chronicling Munster history from before St Patrick until 1092, with additions to 1326; the *Book of Ballymote* – translations of classical texts, Gaelic history, legend and genealogy (about 1390); the *Yellow Book of Lecan* – a confection transcribed from 1391 onwards from the family library of the hereditary historians (*sennachies*), the MacFirBhisigh of Lecan, County Sligo. Spiky minuscule was pressed into service for *Foras Feasa ar Éirinn* or 'Foundation of Knowledge on Ireland', a history of Ireland down to the twelfth century written by the scholar G. Keating (1576-1644) and circulated in manuscript among nationalist connoisseurs.

Carolingian reform

Carolingian minuscule script originated in the writing departments of continental monasteries such as Luxeuil, Corbie and Tours during the eighth century. The script was officially adopted by the Frankish royal court of Pepin III and the Holy Roman Emperor Charlemagne, traditionally through the influence of the English scholar Alcuin, who served Charlemagne from 781. The palaeographical term 'Carolingian' (or 'Caroline') derives from Carolus Magnus, the Latin form of the name of Charlemagne (Charles the Great). The novel minuscule handwriting, synthesised from the various regional styles of continental western Europe, attained its classic form at Tours around 830. In the wake of monastic reform, the script was adopted in England by monks at Winchester around 960 and spread to the Canterbury monastic school by 1020, to Wales by 1120, then to southern Scotland, but not to Ireland. Carolingian was used in religious, literary, business and gov-

Characteristic letter-forms of Carolingian script.

This scene from the Bayeux Tapestry shows the death of King Harold. The inscription in Carolingian capital letters reads (in Latin) HAROLD REX INTERFECTUS EST, 'King Harold is killed'.

35

ernment records. Carolingian was the basis of the hand of Domesday Book, influenced later medieval text, business and charter hands, and ultimately supplied a model for Roman typefaces of modern printing. Carolingian, upright, uniform and symmetrical, achieved its clarity from a separation of letters (except in a few ligatures *st*, *ct*, *nt*, *et*) and its beauty from a consistent roundness of letter-form. Serifs were understated. Punctuation was indicated by single stops. Certain Latin words were abbreviated: *archi epo.* for *archiepiscopo*; & for *et*; *omnib.* for *omnibus*; *ptinentibus* for *pertinentibus*. Carolingian acquired a fount of large initial letters, essentially Roman capital letters.

In English scripts the *a* was rounded; the ascender of *d* stood erect; the bow of *e* was closed; *g* was round with a curved tail; *r* took its small shouldered form; *s* took its long form, standing on the line and raising a high ascender with rightward-curving top (superficially resembling *f*); *t* continued flat-headed and round-bottomed.

qui propter delictum nobilitatem perdit

This early example of printing in Roman-style typeface dates from 1468. The Latin reads 'who loses renown on account of transgression'.

Book hand

Medieval book hand for formal writing sprang from Carolingian stock. Scribes condensed Carolingian letters into narrow stiff perpendicularity, adopting an obliquely cut broad quill to impart an authoritative weight and blackness. Vertical strokes became emphatic **minims** (the single vertical penstrokes forming such letters as m and u). Curves sharpened into angles, oblique strokes faded to hairlines.

Ascenders and descenders were truncated. Densely written pages of this formal script suggested to scholars a woven textile, hence the terms used by palaeographers for the script, **textus**, **textualis** or **textura** from the Latin word *texere*, 'to weave'. Textus is also commonly known as **gothic script** in the sense of medieval or old-fashioned.

michi panes die ac nocte

A high-grade book hand of around 1490 of the variety known as 'textus quadratus'. The Latin reads 'michi panes die ac nocte' meaning '[give] to me bread by day and night'.

36

A regular right-hand margin for each column and page was achieved by word-breaking at the end of the line; by judicious use of abbreviation to complete the line, column or page; by fusing adjacent letters so that oc, od, bo, po, might share a downstroke and save a minim. Around 1250 two forms of textus could be distinguished: **quadratus** (with diamond-shaped serif at the head and hairline tick at the foot) and **prescissus** (with legs squared off footless at the base).

A book hand of 1340, of the highest grade and in the 'textus prescissus' form. The Latin reads 'Quoniam spiritus', meaning 'because the spirit'.

Characteristic letter-forms include *a* with top bow closed from 1250; *d* upright around 1100, mixed indiscriminately with uncial *d* around 1200; straight and round *r* equally acceptable; round *s* replacing long *s* in terminal position. Capital letters (evolved for headings, initials and seal inscriptions) developed generous uncial forms (*H* and *M* as early as Domesday Book). Cabriole-legged *N* and round-bottomed *T* married influences from their minuscule contemporaries and their uncial forebears.

The Gothic book hand was the normal script for prestige items such as a Bible. Particularly popular were illustrated psalters (books of the Psalms) and books of hours (containing prayers to be said at particular hours of the day). The gothic script was used for captions to wall paintings, wax seals on documents, memorial brasses, stained glass win-

dows and funeral hatchments (wooden boards painted with the heraldic coats of arms of deceased persons displayed in the parish church). Monastic **cartularies** (registers containing copies of title deeds) might be written in a more relaxed version of the Gothic book hand.

The most opulent texts were embellished with borders of twining foliage inhabited by mythical and real birds and beasts and with finely painted **versals** (decorative initials, sometimes known as illuminated letters). Headings, directions for the conduct of

37

Illuminated versal reading 'DEUS IN' ('O God in') introducing the prayers known as Prime (to be recited at dawn), from a book of hours written about 1325. The picture depicts a medieval story in which the boy Jesus turns a group of children into swine.

divine service and important passages of the text were lettered in red ink. This is known as **rubrication** from the Latin word *rubrica*, 'red ochre'. The word 'rubric' came eventually to denote any heading, but especially one offering legal or religious instruction, and any entry in a church calendar giving a saint's name. In its English form, 'red-letter', the word is still applied to significant, or red-letter, days in our lives.

incomprehensibile

The word 'incomprehensibile' set out in a printer's Gothic type in 1497.

The Gothic book hand remained in regular use throughout the middle ages. The script, written large, bold and black, came to be associated with mourning or with inauspicious times – hence 'black-letter' days. Early printers, such as William Caxton, who set up his press at Westminster in 1476, used a typeface based on Gothic book hand, now usually referred to as black-letter type.

'The ma[n] is blest [tha]t heth not be[n]t, to wicked red his...' This is the beginning of Psalm 1 (the word 'red' means 'counsel'). The handwriting is Gothic book hand, accompanying the tenor part of a metrical psalter written by Thomas Wood, vicar of St Andrews in 1566.

Business hands to 1290

Early business hands, the fluent practical sisters of strait-laced book hand, were developed for the ordinary business of the clerk in government, the church or commerce. The word 'clerk' here reminds us that literate individuals were then generally churchmen (in other words clergymen, clerics or clerks for short). The busiest clerks were, perhaps, those working in the departments and courts of government. Here were written the official administrative records (properly termed **archives**) which enshrine the indispensable collective memory of government. The various scripts of government clerks are referred to as **departmental** or **court** hands, because a number of the oldest departments of government organised their business on the lines of a court of justice.

An important duty of the secretarial department, the Court of Chancery, was the recording of evidence relating to the title or ownership of property in documents consequently known as **title deeds**. Chancery also issued **writs** or **charters**. The writ was, in its eleventh-century form, a notification to officials of the English shire (including bishop and sheriff) that a grant of property or privilege had been made. It was a short-form statement including the names of the people involved, a description of the property or privilege granted and a note of payments and conditions. It was an open letter with a seal attached for authentication and was intended for the information of all concerned both present and future. The term continues in use down to the present to encompass many kinds of formal writings, especially title deeds, court papers and crown summonses. By the twelfth century the writ was generally issued in modified form as a charter (from the Roman word *charta*, 'a papyrus leaf', and, by extension, any short message written on paper). The word simply means a legal document. For this reason business or court hand is often known as **charter hand**.

A charter hand of around 1170: 'ego Ricard[us] de Merebira' meaning 'I, Richard of Marbury'.

Typically, the business clerk wrote rapidly, the small round plain hand acquiring a slight leftward slope. The ascenders of *b h k l* exhibited a small tag near top left from late in the eleventh century. Ascender heads also curled rightwards (from about 1150), imparting a split, notched or bifurcated (forked) finish. Around 1230 ascender heads curled further, to become looped and increasingly floreated down to the end of the century. Reforms in penmanship during the thirteenth century produced pronounced thickening of horizontal and diagonal strokes, notably in the left-ward-slanting ascender of *d*, beaver-tailed *g* and *S*, and the arching mark inscribed above an abbreviated word. Initial letter-forms were dignified from the late twelfth century onwards by the addition of vertical chords to *B C D E G O P Q R T* and by doubling of cross-strokes in *A H M N*. Characteristic letter-forms included *a* with a curving ascender (around 1230) which curled over (by 1280) to form a double bow; superscript (written above the line) *a* topped by an extended horizontal stroke, perhaps with tail waving in the air; *B* confusable with *H*; *e* rotund and beginning to revolve to a dormant posture; *h* dangling a right foot below the line; *r* taking shouldered form (perhaps with descending stem in insular minuscule manner) and round form especially following a rounded letter (originally only *o*, but from around 1210 after *b d p*); small *s* used terminally from about 1150, in any position after 1250, but rarely medially after 1290; traditional long *s* employed in all positions down to 1290 and thereafter ceasing to appear terminally.

Characteristic
letter-
forms of
business
hands to
1290.

A a a a   B b b b

C D d E e G g H h

k l N O P Q

R r r S s s T

Business hands 1290-1330

During the generation 1290-1330 business hand achieved a compact bureaucratic clarity. The hand was written large and upright. Exaggerated horizontals, diagonals and beaver-tailings declined. Floreation withered. Ascenders were topped by a simple rightward hook or loop (or occasionally a vestige of a notch). Descenders were long, plain and tapering (except *g*, which took small double-decker form, and *f p s*,

f   g   i   M   N

p   r   r   long s

Characteristic letter-forms of business hands from 1290 to 1330.

which could be looped to their left). The accent on *i* was curved and distinctive. *M* and *N* shed their multiple crossbars to become small and rounded. Cabriole-legged (enlarged minuscule) *N* was particularly cursive, with looped descender. The rounded form of *r* acquired a tail at its base while, in the shouldered form, the lowering of the point from which the shoulder sprang culminated in the disappearance of the shoulder itself.

Business hand 1330-70

This looped and rounded writing developed under the hands of the succeeding generation of clerks. Young scribes, less disciplined (or perhaps more busy) than their writing masters, lapsed into cursive habits. Test letters from this period (1330-70) included new-style *e* written in a single penstroke and rolled on to its back; an old style *e* sometimes closing into a circle; an *i* whose curved accent closed into a circle or was linked in a flourish to the letter-foot.

e   e   i

Characteristic letter-forms of business hands from 1330 to 1370.

Mongrel hand 1370-1525

Mongrel script (sometimes referred to as **bastard** hand) was a merger of book hand with cursive business hand under the influ-

A charter of 1390: Anno d[omi]ni mill[es]i[m]o CCC^{mo} Nonagesimo ∴, meaning 'in the one thousandth three hundredth ninetieth year of the Lord'. This is mongrel script used for a formal document.

41

ence of Flemish, Burgundian and French masters. The professional **scriveners** (copyists) of London (incorporated as a guild by 1357) were among the first writers in England to use the script. These clerks (known as *scriptores littere curialis*, 'writers of the court letter') served not only courts of law but private business and public administration. They were thus well placed to ensure that the implanted seed of writing reform would flourish. Various versions of the mongrel script were employed for a century and more by merchants for commercial letters and accounts; by administrators for the management of estates and kingdoms; and by ecclesiastical clerks for wills and bishop's registers. Professional

The beginning of an address written in England in the French language in 1471 in mongrel hand: 'Tres hault et puissant prince' meaning 'very high and mighty prince'.

copyists were kept busy as the demand for books grew apace. Religious texts headed the bestseller list, though these could be of tiresome length, and the clerk tasked to reproduce the disquisitions of **schoolmen** (university lecturers in theology) might well be forgiven a personal colophon to punctuate the learned peroration:

Explicit secunda pars summe fratris thome de aquino
ordinis fratrum predicatorum, longissima,
prolixissima, et tediosissima scribenti; Deo gratias,
Deo gratias, et iterum Deo gratias.

The copyist's outburst on completing his task may be (freely) translated:

The second part of the treatise of Brother

Thomas Aquinas of the Black Friars expounds

in the longest, most prolix and tedious manner;

thank God, thank God, and again thank God!

Popular medieval bestsellers, too, were copied by hand. Shorter romances such as *Sir Gawain and the Green Knight* and *Troilus and Cressida* each ran to well over 2000 lines of copying; Langland's *Piers Plowman* was nearly three times that length, as was the English abridgement of the *Romaunt of the Rose*. Chaucer's *Canterbury Tales* extended to some seventeen thousand lines of verse and prose.

Mongrel script might be written freely, cursively, carelessly and currently (joined up). It was employed for workaday writings: by

Characteristic letter forms of mongrel hand.

a B b C d d

E e f G g h

i k l p q long r

S long s T yogh

the parish priest for his homilies; by the student of the Temple for his lecture notes. The clerk of Oxenford spent long hours in university, cathedral and convent libraries copying in his own free mongrel hand the books he required for study but could not afford to buy. Common folk conducted familiar correspondence in a rapid rightward-sloped mongrel **free hand**, for instance the famous Paston letters, some hundreds of family letters spanning the eventful reigns of Henry V, Henry VI, Edward IV, Richard III and Henry VII.

The mongrel script demonstrated character traits of both parents. From Gothic book hand the mongrel inherited an upright stance, reticence in the use of ties, and angularity which infected the curves of *a b B C d e q*. Capital letters *B C E G S* were rounded and embellished with vertical strokes and perhaps a central dot; *T* was considerably convoluted. The mongrel inherited a businesslike simplicity: descenders of *f p q*, long *r* and long *s* were straight and tapering to a point. Serifs were rare, but heads and feet of minims might be finished with a tiny hook. A rightward hook topped the ascenders of *b h k l*, developing subsequently into an angular loop. Characteristic letters of mongrel script were *a* in its several forms; *d*, though rivalled from around 1400 by a cursive looped form with diagonal stroke; *g* and long-tailed *h* developing in currency; *i* with or without a dot, a hairstroke, or circular accent. Spiky *yogh* (derived from flat-topped *g*) was used at the end of English words which later were terminated with the two letters 'gh', such as 'bough' and 'thorough'. By 1500 *yogh* was considered old-fashioned.

43

Splayed hand, a mongrel script and a forerunner of later business scripts, was so named because its letters (without ascenders or descenders) suffered compression from top and bottom and were thus squeezed or splayed sideways. Descenders were curtailed. Minims sloped to the left while the tie-strokes sloped to the right, providing an effect like the teeth of a saw. Distinctive letters were *e g p* and *x* (a current and confusable single penstroke), *r* (of the Gothic variety, though with round *r* also common), *t* (taller than c, and crossed).

c	e	g	p	r	r	t	x

Characteristic letter-forms of splayed hand.

Splayed hand version of 'kyng Eduard ye iiijth'.

Departmental set hands

The set or departmental hands were evolved by and peculiar to the departments (courts) of central government. Their scripts are alternatively described as **court hands**. Written with a high (50°) pen angle, the scripts varied little from clerk to clerk (or from century to century) within each department. Much of the business of clerks in government lay in **engrossing**, that is, fair copying of documents in a large formalised script for legal or administrative purposes. Everyone in an office was taught to engross in the same script.

The script of the Exchequer **Pipe Office** (perhaps so named because its collections of rolled-up documents looked like pipes) was the first set hand. Pipe Office hand reflected in its large bold letters the awe which kings, clerks and commoners felt for the large parchment pipe rolls recording (from the twelfth century onwards) the crown's dealings with sheriffs and debtors. With

Pipe Office hand, 1628: 'sub no[m]i[n]e ciuiu[m] Norwic' meaning 'under the name of the city of Norwich'.

proud disregard for handwriting developments outside the office, clerks dispensed with the minims of *m n u* while accentuating the serifs. A line of writing was thus created which was characterised by sequences of paired diamond-shaped dots (a vestige of serifs) punctuated by recognisable letters and by *i* reduced to three dots (two serifs with a dot above). Clerks embellished the capitals of much-repeated phrases such as *Summa*, meaning 'sum total' and *Et quietus est,* 'And he is quit', that is, his account is paid in full.

Other sections of the Exchequer adopted distinctive departmental hands from about 1480 onwards under the influence of mongrel script. Palaeographers recognise the characteristic scripts of the divisions of the **King's Remembrancer** and **Lord Treasurer's Remembrancer**.

Exchequer (King's Remembrancer) hand 1642: 'corne grayne and malt'.

Chancery hand, another mongrel development, achieved its distinctive identity by about 1480. It was employed for documents issued under the monarch's great seal, for letters patent, original writs and miscellaneous enrolments. Links between minims were from the first only faintly drawn at the base, vanishing altogether during the sixteenth century. Gothic *e* was preferred.

Chancery hand in England, 1562: 'the said Sir Thomas'.

Court hand (Scottish Chancery), 1641: 'vndecem libras duos solidos duos denarios' meaning £11 2s 2d.

The hands of the English courts of **King's Bench** and **Common Pleas** (developed from the late fifteenth century) were extensively employed by lawyers in London and the provinces for legal documents such as fines, recoveries,

The hand of the English Court of Common Pleas in 1508: 'finalis concordia' meaning 'the concluding agreement'.

This is an illustration of Chancery and other legal hands from A. Wright, 'Court Hand Restored', 1776. This is one of the earliest palaeographical textbooks, published when all the medieval scripts were fading from the memory of scholars.

title deeds, memoranda and commonplace books. These court hands were upright, though perhaps sloping leftwards in late examples. Letter-forms were tall and thin. Emphatic ascenders and descenders traced crescentic curves below and (less often) above the line. Vertical strokes through the capitals *C E G* and *Q* developed a dagger-sharp form, at first piercing through the base and later projecting above the top of the letter.

In 1650 the use of the set hands (and Latin) was discontinued in favour of 'an ordinary, usual, and legible hand and character and not in any hand commonly called court hand'. This revolutionary remedy for bureaucratic mystification was, however, short-lived, and departmental hands were restored, along with the king, in 1660. Departmental hands were next abolished from 1733 under an act of 1731 which specified that court records 'shall be written in such a common legible Hand and Character, as the Acts of Parliament are usually ingrossed in . . . and not in any Hand commonly called *Court Hand* and in Words at Length and not abbreviated'.

Secretary hand

Secretary script developed by 1525 from a splayed version of mongrel hand. Secretary could be written rapidly and currently (though in its most current form legibility was sacrificed to speed).

Secretary stood erect at first, gradually developing an accelerative rightward slope. The slope was seldom consistent; double *f* and double long *s* leaned in opposite directions, and *A* leaned backwards against the flow. Letters *i m n u* were refined to their bare minims, though *u* might be distinguished by a sagging mark above, and *i* by its dot. Characteristic letters were *a c g* with attacking stroke; *c* and *t* perhaps scarcely distinguishable, a mere minim with horizontal cross-stroke; *d*, a backward-curving single stroke; *e* high and laid back in splayed style; *h* (the typical secretary letter) an unruly straggling descender; *k* conspicuously involved; *p* (and *x*) a single economical penstroke; *r* (in classic secretary) splayed open, though a diminutive round form continued; terminal *s* with round belly and tail held high; *v* (as *b*) raising an ascender; doubled ascenders to create *w*.

From the vulgar secretary, writing-masters refined a dignified variant known as **engrossing secretary** to compete with established departmental hands for formal purposes, notably for documents written in English. Engrossing secretary was notably upright with few links between letters and few abbreviations. There was a clear contrast between the main and the subsidiary strokes of letters such as *m* and *w*.

Secretary was taught by professional writing-masters. The

earliest writing-master's copybook was *A Booke Containing Divers Sortes of Hands* (1570) by J. de Beauchesne and J. Baildon, followed by *A Newe Book of Copies* (1574), and *Petie Schole* (1587) by F. Clement.

Characteristic letter-forms of secretary hand as illustrated in J. de Beauchesne and J. Baildon, 'A Booke containing Divers Sortes of Hands', 1570.

More people were writing than ever before. Central government clerks in the pay of Renaissance kings and queens laid the foundations of the modern bureaucratic centralised state. Local government (justices of the peace, parish constables and borough officials) became a power in the land. Large numbers of ordinary people now actually wrote letters and diaries, confiding their personal thoughts to paper. Secretary was the everyday hand of John Knox and William Shakespeare.

Humanistic hand

Humanistic script was invented by scholars of the fifteenth century who claimed to be students of human nature rather than old-fashioned theologians. The humanists were men of the Renaissance, a period of rebirth of interest in the world of ancient Greece and Rome. Humanistic script is thus sometimes also known as *littera antiqua* or simply *antica*, implying letter-forms of the ancient world. Because the script was invented in Italy it is also sometimes (and confusingly) known as **italic** script. It was a reformed version of the Carolingian minuscule used in the Holy Roman Empire of Charlemagne (around AD 800).

Humanistic script is a neat non-current, perhaps serifed, upright script, initially adopted as a legible book hand. A sloped humanistic hand (of Italian invention and so known as italic) penetrated the Vatican to enter papal briefs (official letters), though not papal bulls, around 1450. In England, humanistic hand was promoted by Peter Carmelianus, Latin secretary to Henry VII. Writers literate in both humanistic and secretary switched between the two, favouring humanistic for a signature, heading, marginal note, biblical allusion or classical quotation (an origin of the modern practice of

Scottish humanistic display script from an ecclesiastical court record of 1666.

italicising such intrusive matter), reserving secretary for the remainder. Humanistic hand (inscribed with an obliquely cut pen held obliquely) employed rounded letter-forms which flowed into looping currency and into decorative excess. Scribes favoured beaded heads for ascenders with swooping coils and loops to descenders.

Characteristic humanistic letters include round, closed, long-tailed *b d p q*; *k* purged of secretary convolutions; *s v w x*; *h* standing with both feet firmly on the line. Fashion required much embellishment to dignify a signature, involve a monogram and decorate a margin or versal.

Humanistic letter-forms were adopted by the first printers from the fifteenth century onwards. To the printer humanistic script is known as Roman type, because of its use of capital letter-forms from ancient Rome. Humanistic lettering is still in use today – indeed this book is printed in a humanistic typeface. In the printer's workshop different trays contained different styles and sizes (**founts**) of type. Traditional type consisted of small rectangular metal blocks each with a single raised (reversed) letter. The printer composed a page of text by selecting letters one by one and fixing them line by line in a frame. Capital letters were selected from an **upper case** of type, small letters from a **lower case**. The block of text was then inked and the image transferred to paper under mechanical pressure in a printing press. And, of course, each page might be printed in thousands.

To some people (not least to professional copyists) printing seemed to spell the end of handwriting: if the newfangled printing press was not controlled, the written word would lose its mystic dignity and people would forget how to write for themselves! Other wiseacres gloomily foresaw the disastrous consequences of placing the printed word in the hands of the common people; what would the world come to if anybody (and everybody) could own and read a Bible or a law book!

Mixed hand

The scribal companionship of secretary and humanistic led inevitably to a closer connection, engendering a crew of handwriting mongrels. The offspring was legitimised by the writing-masters of the seventeenth century as English **round hand**, though persistently betraying mixed parentage. Looped humanistic *d* and secretary *d* were employed interchangeably in the same document. Italic *h* stood cheek by jowl with secretary *e*. As round hand came of age during the eighteenth century, the script assumed a consistent

This business card from the nineteenth century has examples of copperplate (lines 1 and 3), Gothic (line 2) and sans serif ('without serifs', line 4).

elegant rightward slope. In its gracious loops and complete currency, mature round hand recommended itself to engravers, the craftsmen who cut pictures and text into metal (usually copper) plates for printing. This application earned the more curvaceous examples of round hand the familiar name of **copperplate** script. Anachronistic long *s* survived into the early twentieth century, though latterly reserved for the first *s* of a double *s* in the writing of old men and conservative eccentrics. The distinction between the consonants *v* and *w* and the vowel *u* was at last established in round hand; the differentiation of *i* (vowel) and *j* (consonant), too, was fixed. Round hands predominated for three centuries until overtaken by the new technology of the typewriter (from around 1880) and the microcomputer (from the 1970s), whose typefaces gave a new lease of life to the old humanistic letter-forms.

Engrossing hand

During the late seventeenth century the formal and upright engrossing secretary script was influenced by sloping italic styles. This resulted in a general engrossing hand for use in a variety of legal documents, particularly after the abolition of departmental

A will copied in engrossing hand in 1819.

set hands. Engrossing hand was upright, though individual tall
letters such as *t* might slope rightwards near their top. Letters were
looped and capital letters were convoluted. The hand was used in
the law until after 1900.

*Words from a deed enrolled in Chancery in 1830 in engrossing hand:
'Llanelly in the County of Carmarthen'.*

Romantic revival and reform

The ascendancy of Roman type and round hand was challenged
by revivalists and reformers. Men of letters reacted against ancient
Greece and Rome to rediscover (and re-invent) the writing of the
middle ages. Wealthy antiquarians amassed collections of ancient
manuscripts, while academic historians recovered the mouldy,
worm-eaten, mouse-gnawed heritage of public records. This archival passion received official sanction through the appointment (in
1764) of Record Commissioners, who encouraged the leading
palaeographers of the time to prepare scholarly editions, cata-
logues (known as **calendars**), transcripts and translations of historical manuscripts of national importance. The commissioners
published in 1802 a catalogue of the Cottonian Library deposited
in the British Museum (a collection of manuscripts which forms
the basis of the British Library's immense collection of documentary treasures). Later they published the *Ancient Laws and Insti-*

In Roelav Hvnd.

Isd.G.ten *Herford*. Dodo tenuit fic lib hō. Ibi. ii. hidæ geld.

Tra.ē. ii. car. Ibi funt. iiii. uilli 7 ii. bord 7 fab. hntes. i. car.

In Wich una falina redd. ii. folid. 7 alia dimidia falina wafta.

Ibi. i. ac pti. De hac tra ten un miles dimid hidā. 7 ibi hē. i.

car. 7 ii. bouar. 7 iii. bord. T.R.E. ualb. xx. fol. Modo. x. folid.

This is the entry for Hartford in Cheshire from the edition of Domesday in record type published by the Record Commissioners in 1783.

tutes of England* (1840) and *Acts of the Parliaments of Scotland, 1124-1707*, illustrated with coloured, printed facsimiles of documents (1814-75). The dedicated typeface designed for printed transcriptions (now known as **record type**) employed a contemporary serifed Roman face, with all the appropriate modified letters and special signs of medieval writing.

The trail pioneered by the Record Commissions was followed by the Public Record Office (established in London in 1838) and, to a lesser extent, by the Irish and Scottish Record Offices. Between 1861 and 1864 the Ordnance Survey published a photographic facsimile of *Domesday Book*, a valuable supplement to the printed record-type edition prepared by A. Farley and published in 1783. Historical societies carried forward the work of transcription and publication. Their work covers a wide range of manuscripts relevant to national and local history including church records, manorial muniments, borough court books and charters. Manuscripts thus available in printed editions are listed in the successive volumes of *Texts and Calendars* (1958 onwards). For the palaeographer these editions offer models for transcription and guides to editorial practice. Published editions also contain illustrations of pages from the handwritten original.

Erse script in modern Ireland

From the seventeenth century onwards, publishers of national texts and Irish language pamphlets preferred printed typefaces derived from the traditional spiky insular minuscule. During the nineteenth century John O'Donovan and E. O'Curry, both officers of the Ordnance Survey and both later professors of Celtic studies, forwarded the cause of the Erse (Irish) script. O'Donovan wrote an informal hand with an ordinary quill to show that anyone could be taught the ancient writing. Between 1922 and 1966 the insular minuscule was adopted in primary schools to accompany the Irish language. Signwriters busily adopted the script as a gesture to new nationhood for shops, post offices and telephone boxes. Irish script was preserved particularly for anti-quarian, literary or religious purposes and to accompany prestig-ious illuminated texts, bilingual grants of arms, diplomatic let-ters of credence and state papers.

Calligraphy

Calligraphy, that is handwriting as an art-form, has flourished down the centuries. The calligrapher seeks to be more than just a competent, legible penman. Indeed, mere legibility may get in the way of the calligrapher's art. Sometimes calligraphic effect is achieved in spite of a text that is trite or commonplace.

Irish illuminators of the dark ages laboured long hours on the calligraphic first page of a gospel book such as the *Book of Kells* (around AD 800). The first words of St John's Gospel, *In principio erat verbum,* 'In the beginning was the word', are presented as a complete calligraphic package of dignified lettering, gorgeous colouring, intricate decoration and imaginative layout – an image for wonder and contemplation as well as a page of sacred text.

Artistic calligraphy as practised during the seventeenth cen-tury (when the word calligraphy was first coined) was the prov-ince of the professional writing-master. A simple written maxim in a basic secretary or humanistic script was tied up in convo-luted coils of pen-drawn loops, paraphs (flourishes) and knot-work in which the pen, miraculously, seemed never to lift from the paper. The writing-master and penman demonstrated flair and technique as art for its own sake and also by way of adver-tisement to would-be pupils.

The growth in the use of the printed word freed imaginative penmen from the hack work of mere copying. During the nine-teenth century, rebelling against the mechanical materialism of the age, penmen sought to rediscover (and to reproduce) the ideal of the handwritten medieval book. The Arts and Crafts move-ment – and especially such multi-talented designers as William Morris – pursued the virtue of beauty through craftsmanship. In book production this meant imaginative new handwriting styles, medieval-style typefaces, elegant limited-edition books, high-quality hand-finished papers and fine bindings. At the close of the nineteenth century the plainer Art Nouveau style of such calligraphers as Walter Crane was influential. This inspired Edward Johnston to write his classic manual of contemporary calligraphy *Writing and Illuminating, and Lettering* (1906).

The nineteenth century was also the heyday of the craftsman signwriter. Booming commerce called for ebullient lettering for shop fronts and billboards. Designers responded to the demand with lettering for every purpose. Joyful playbill lettering was embraced as the style appropriate to the fairground and the circus. Gothic-style lettering was deemed suitable for stained-glass windows in restored parish churches. Shopfitters and advertisers were able to choose from an expanding plethora of fancy founts.

Anglo-Norman clerks in the service of William the Conqueror compiled Domesday Book of 1086 in a practical administrative version of Carolingian script. This extract (in Latin) refers to Guildford, Surrey.

3
Abbreviation

Systems of abbreviation were introduced into old handwritings to assist both writer and reader. The nature of the abbreviation was suggested by symbols, signs or modified letters.

The Romans devised thousands of abbreviations to help the businessman write his letters more quickly and the law clerk to take down the spoken evidence of witnesses. Shorthand, systems of speed-writing using symbols and shortened words, was extensively adopted by government clerks to keep up with the administrative needs of the expanding empire. Monumental inscriptions on stone were heavily abbreviated so that a long message could be conveyed by the minimum of carving.

Abbreviations were known to the ancient Romans as *litterae singulares*, 'special letter-forms', and were publicised through the writings of grammarians. From the imperial epoch there emerged three important systems of abbreviation: firstly, the literary or secretarial system of Tiro; secondly, the legal system; thirdly, the Christian system.

autem

contra

The first system was reputedly invented by Tiro, the freedman and secretary of the famous orator Cicero. Words and syllables in frequent use were expressed by simple symbols known as **tironian notes**. This was a true shorthand **substituting** a symbol for a whole word.

enim

The legal profession adopted a system known as 'legal symbols' (Latin, *notae juris*). These were taught through legal textbooks. Abbreviation consisted, firstly, of the initial letters of a word or syllable. This kind of abbreviation is described as a **suspension**, just as modern writers still write 'i.e.' for the Latin words *id est*, meaning 'that is to say', and MS for the English word 'manuscript'. Roman lawyers adopted a second strategy in respect of recurring final syllables, words or phrases. These were represented by either a symbol or a single letter written above the line of writing, known as a **superscript** letter. The common Latin word-ending '-*mus*' was thus shown as *m*; *modo*, 'now', was written *m°*.

est

et

et

Abbreviations used by the Romans.

56

patti	(pat·ti) patrati XV	*pḃe*	(pbe) praebe-re XIV m.
pau.deℓea3	(paudeLeaz) Paulus de Leazaris (abbr. giur.) XV	*pḃē*	(pbe) probem XIV
p·aug.	(PAug) Praefectus Augustalis	*pḃe~*	(pber) probetur XIV p.
ṗb3	(pb) praebet XIV m.	*p̃bꞮḃ3*	(pᵃbⁱᵇ) praedica-bilibus XIV p.
p̄b3	(pb) praebent XIV m.	*pḃℓc*	(pblc) publice XII f.
pb3	(pb) probet XIV	*pḃℓē̃b3*	(pbleᵃᵇ) problema-tibus XIV
pb3	(pb) probus IX	*pḃℓɩcõ*	(pblico) publica-tionem XV
pḃᶜᶜ	(pbᶜᶜ) publi-cae XIV f,	*p̄b̃n̄ⁱˢ*	(pbnⁱˢ) praeben-dis XIII
pḃº	(pbº) proba-tio XIII f.	*pḃō*	(pbo) probatio XIII f.
p̃ḃʳ	(pᵃbʳ) probabi-liter XIV p.	*pḃom*	(pbom) probatio-nem XIV
pḃ²ᶜ	(pbʳ) probrum XIV f.	*pḃoñ*	(pbon) probatio-nem XIV
pḃaᵎ	(pbaʳ) proban-tur XV m.	P.B.P.O.	(PBPO) Post beatorum pedum oscula XVI p.
pḃaⁿ	(pbaʳ) proba-biliter XV m.	*PB̃R*	(PBR) Presbyter (*nei sigilli*) XII
ꞙat	(pbat) probat XIII	*pḃr*	(pbr) presbyter XII m.
pbaꞇ̄	(pbat) probatum XV	*pḃrº*	(pbrº) presbyte-ro XIV f.
p̄baꞇ⁹	(pbat) presbyte-ratus XIII	*pḃratuɠ*	(pbratus) presbyteratus (scr. bull.) XVII

A page from Cappelli's 'Dizionario di Abbreviature', 1899.

Early Christians used abbreviations for sacred names (*nomina sacra*). This was usually achieved by **contraction**, reducing a word to a few significant letters: *dominus*, 'Lord', as *DNS*; *deus*, 'God', as *DS*; *ihesus*, as *ihs*. A horizontal stroke above the abbreviated form indicated that an abbreviation had taken place.

Systems of abbreviation had to be learned correctly or the wrong message might be sent. There was no standard dictionary of abbreviation for the Roman writer and so confusion doubtless occurred from time to time. In the fifth and sixth centuries abbreviation was banned in official writings. This ban did not apply to business or literary writing, though in practice abbreviation faded from these kinds of writing too. By the ninth century the Roman systems of abbreviation were just a dim memory. However, administrators, lawyers, grammarians and theologians could not resist a small abbreviation now and then to ease the tedium of hand copying. By the era of Domesday Book in England (1086) abbreviation was back in fashion and flourishing as a sophisticated system.

For the palaeographer interested in medieval abbreviations the indispensable dictionary-guides are C. T. Martin, *The Record Interpreter* (third edition, 1982) and A. Cappelli, *Dizionario di Abbreviature Latine ed Italiane* (1899, reprinted 1967). The introductions to both these books explain how they, perforce, differ in their arrangement from an ordinary dictionary. Arrangement is complicated by having to include letters of the alphabet in both unamended and amended forms. Martin's book is especially useful because it contains (in addition to a dictionary of abbreviations) a glossary of Latin words, forms of English place-names, surnames and Christian names, and the Latin names of bishoprics in England, Wales, Scotland and Ireland. Cappelli offers a comprehensive dictionary of abbreviations with the added bonus for palaeographers of a list in which the abbreviated forms are in facsimile (that is the original handwriting) rather than in standardised record-type transliteration.

For the beginner the medieval system of abbreviation can be simplified down to nine principal signs and four additional special uses. These thirteen principals reflect the essence of abbreviation strategies used by British and Irish writers from the twelfth century to the nineteenth.

1. This pervasive mark of abbreviation took the usual form of a horizontal, straight, arched or sagging line perhaps with a curling end. The sign might be long, overlining the whole word; or short, indicating the specific point of abbreviation. The sign was drawn above, below or through letters according to its

Sign	Nine marks of abbreviation			
1	～　⌒　－　＼　＿　～　🝆			
2	～　⌐		6	𝟫
3	𝄚　𝞪		7	⸵　𝔧　𝔧
4	𝟫　ꞯ　ſ		8	𝓁　ſ
5	𝔂　𝟫		9	𝓁　ſ　ƥ

These nine symbols of abbreviation have been used in documents (medieval and modern) to represent omitted letters.

particular application. The basic sign was elaborated according to scribal whim, notably into the papal knot affected by a generation of writers around 1200. In general use the sign abbreviated place-names and all manner of frequently recurring words. The sign was especially useful for indicating the omission of *i, m* or *n*; *er, ar* and *or.*

d̄n̄o ēp d̄c̄s
d[omi]no ep[iscopus] d[i]c[tu]s
'to the lord' 'bishop' 'the said'

sacramͤtum fratrū totā
sacram[en]tum fratru[m] tota[m]
'oath' 'brother' 'all'

lībͣa ƥish tempͤe
lib[er]a p[ar]ish temp[or]e
'free'   'in the time'

2. This sign comprised a horizontal line with a hook to the left drawn through the descender of *p*, specifically representing *pro* (in Latin or English).

3. This was originally a superscript ^{r} but was, from 1150, applied specifically to indicate the omission of *er*, *ar*, *re*, *ra* and (more occasionally) *ir*, *or*. Above *p* the sign always denoted *pre*. In general application the sign was rendered as a diminutive superior comma and/or attached by a flourish to a terminal letter. In medieval Latin writings this symbol is seen hanging above the end of personal names and place-names as a mark of suspension, saving the scribe from having to decide which Latin termination might be appropriate for English, Celtic and Norman names. Printers and round-hand writers elevated this comma to hang over a range of English abbreviations and possessives: can't, shan't, fear'd, it's, won't, I'm, surpriz'd, man's.

Jur *dd* *vouch*

Jur[atores] d[eman]d[er] vouch[er]
'the jurors' 'to demand' 'to vouch'

4. A little round sign with a broken tail hung above suspensions and contractions to indicate *ur* and terminal *tur*. The same sign with *p* represented *pur* and *pour* in French writing.

p *auditis* *contine*

p[our] audit[ur]is contine[tur]
'for' 'to those 'it is enclosed'
about to be
heard'

5. This was a round superior mark with a curved tail. As a suspension or, more rarely, a contraction, the sign stood for *us* in *eiusdem*, *tempus*, *opus*, but following *p* represented *post*.

ei sdem *temp* *op*

ei[u]sdem temp[us] op[us]
'of itself' 'time' 'work'

6. This sign was inscribed in the line of writing (not superscript) and represented the syllables *con* or *com* in Latin words and also, though more rarely, in English words.

9trouersie
[con]troversie
'controversy'

9 firmation
[con]firmation
'confirmation'

7. Resembling a modern semicolon in twelfth-century writing, this sign developed cursively by the fourteenth century into a long-tailed *z*. The sign stood on the line to indicate suspension: of terminal *us* in Latin, where *bus* was written simply as bz; of the suffix *que,* 'and', written as *qz*; of *verch* (Welsh for 'daughter') written *vz*; and of Latin words ending in *et*. The sign actually survives in modern usage as *viz*, which is an abbreviation of the Latin *videlicet* meaning 'that is to say' or 'namely'; also *oz* as an abbreviation of 'ounce'.

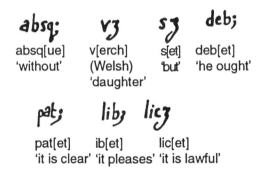

absq;   *v3*   *s3*   *deb;*
absq[ue]   v[erch]   s[et]   deb[et]
'without'   (Welsh)   'but'   'he ought'
             'daughter'

pat;   *lib;*   *lic3*
pat[et]   ib[et]   lic[et]
'it is clear' 'it pleases' 'it is lawful'

8. This obliquely curving mark suspended a word by slashing through the final stroke (especially of *k R r*). This sign was favoured for Latin genitive plurals in *um*. The suspension for *Recipe*, 'receive', is still used today for pharmacists' prescriptions.

animar   *R*
animar[um]   R[ecipe]
'of the souls' 'Receive!'

9. This vertical stroke stood from the fourteenth century onwards as a nonspecific indicator of suspension following letters with ascenders or descenders, notably *d f g*. The sign stood for *es* and *is* in Latin. The sign also stood for *es*, *is*, *ys* and *s* plural and possessive terminations in Middle English writings.

q[uo]d   comit[is]
'that'   'of the earl'

10. Informal shorthand abbreviations in the manner of the modern IOU ('I owe you') peppered writings of all times. Although Shakespeare is not recorded as writing '2B or not 2B', he would almost certainly have used X^r for December: the Roman numeral X for 'ten' (December originally the tenth month) with final r from the English word.

11. Special signs substituted for complete words, for instance the revived tironian note ÷ standing for *est* (1120-1240). Another tironian note stood for the Latin word *et* 'and', and also to the present day for *agus*, meaning 'and' in Irish writing. Two letters might be joined together by an attaching stroke known as a ligature – perhaps so closely linked as to look like a single symbol. This was commonly done for the pairs of letters *ct*, *ft* and *st*. Most common of all was the *et* ligature, particularly in Latin *et* meaning 'and'. This survives today as the & sign, known as ampersand (a word whose meaning is not satisfactorily explained).

12. An initial letter (perhaps with a dot) is another type of abbreviation still in use today. Medievally (as even nowadays) this was most commonly used for Christian names: *Willelmus* (Latin form of William) was abbreviated as *W*. This kind of abbreviation may be referred to by the Latin word *sigla*, 'signs'. Typical examples include *h* for *hoc*, 'this'; *R.* for *Rex*, 'King'; *R.* for *rotulus*, 'a (parchment) roll'; *T.* for *teste*, 'bearing witness'; *.s.* for *scilicet*, 'namely'; *.i.* and *i.e.* for *id est*; *c.c.* for *Cú Chulainn* (the name of a mythical Irish hero); *D.G.REX F.D.* for *Dei Gratia Rex Fidei Defensor*, 'By the grace of God, King, Defender of the Faith'.

13. Superscript letters represented either a terminal or an important medial character in an abbreviated word. In secretary writing

superscript ^{o} indicated *io* or *tio* in nat^{o}nal, ra^{o}nal for national, rational. Any appropriate letter might be superscribed: g^a, *erga*, towards; w^c, which; u^i, *ubi*, where; g^i, *igitur*, therefore; m^r, master; m^{rs}, mistress; w^iin, within. Superscript abbreviation in names gave W^m, J^{no}, *Alex^r*, *Marg^t*. Northern pronunciation preferred *quh* for 'wh' in *quhair*, 'where', *quhilk* 'which', *quhom* 'whom', *quhat* 'what': these generally appeared in abbreviated form as q^r, q^{lk}, q^m, q^t. Combinations of superscription with thorn-derived y gave y^t, y^r *from*, y^r *to* for 'that', 'therefrom', 'thereto'.

Provincial physicians and pharmacists employed medical abbreviations. Mrs Hossack's R[ecipe] (prescription) specifies Ext[ractum] Belladon[nae] (processed deadly nightshade) ʒiv (4 drachms) Sig[netur] (let it be labelled) Belladonna.

4
Numbers

In the ancient world, where writing was invented, numbers were written by means of simple strokes or (in Mesopotamia) dots. The Egyptians wrote numbers up to one million using only seven different signs: for one, ten, one hundred, one thousand, ten thousand, one hundred thousand and one million. Multiples were written by repetition of the relevant sign.

The Romans took on elements of the various number systems in use in the ancient world. They used simple strokes, for example, I, II, III for 1, 2, 3. For numerals 5 and 10 the Romans borrowed a couple of letters from the Chalcidian (Greek) alphabet, which in time came to be conventionally written as the Roman letters V and X. For the larger numbers 100, 1000 and 50 the Romans used three other Chalcidian letters, soon transmuted into recognisable Roman letters.

C = 100 (influenced by Latin *centum*, 100)

M = 1000 (influenced by *mille,* 1000).

L = 50 (Latin, *quinquaginta*, not influenced by any initial letter)

D = 500 (Latin, *quingenti*; written as part of the *mille* sign and conventionalised as **D**.

Medieval writers adopted the Roman system of numerals, though often preferring lower-case letters and a terminal j. Scribes preferred forms such as iiij (four) and xiiij (fourteen); the alternative forms iv and xiv were not usual.

Dates were expressed in Roman numerals. Hundreds were shown by means of a superscript ^{c} (for centum), thus jMv^{c}xxv (1525). Secretary writers in Scotland wrote this Latinism so that the *millesimo* jM, '1000', element appeared as a currently written jaj: thus jajv^{c}xxv was read as 1000, 500, 20 and 5 (1525).

Larger quantities were generally expressed in scores, indicated by

This account of the bishop's tithes is written in the secretary script of the middle of the seventeenth century.
'Firstly upon the Bishop of Moray for eleven chalders nine bolls [of grain] as tithe [valued] at £12 6s 8d the chalder is £142 12s 1d'.

superscript ˣˣ (for twenty). For example iiijˣˣ (fourscore, that is, 80); viijˣˣ (eight score, 160). Occasional confusion may be caused to the modern reader by the application of c to represent the medieval long hundred of six score (one hundred and twenty), where ccl stood for two hundred and ninety (l is 50). In this usage one hundred was written 11 (double l is 2 x 50 or vˣˣ).

Ordinals (first, second, third, seventh, etc.) were expressed by means of superscript letters which, in Latin writings, would change according to case: iijᵃ, *tertia*, 'third'; xjᵐᵒ, *undecimo*, 'eleventh' or '11th'; vijⁱᵉⁿˢ, *septiens*, 'seven times'. Specimen transcription VI is a commentary on *prima secundae,* 'the first half of the second part' of *Summa Theologiae* – numbered 1a2ae in the published edition.

Rapid calculation with Roman numerals was effected by **abacus** systems. The most common abacus consisted of a frame of wires on which beads were threaded.

Exchequer, the financial department of government, took its name from the chequered cloth upon which clerks made calculations and controlled the nation's finances by moving counters up, down and sideways in a grand game of fiscal chess. Merchants and auditors also adopted abacus systems for calculations in the margins of documents expressing sums of money by ink dots arranged in grids and files representing hundreds, tens, units, pounds, shillings, pennies, halfpennies and farthings.

Arabic numerals originated in India and were publicised by the mathematician Al-Khawarizmi. His name, in the form **algorism**, is applied to the system which spread throughout Europe during the eleventh century, entering England around 1200. Medieval writers adopted Arabic numerals for certain marginal and specialised purposes, for example for numbering pages in a codex and for writing the year of grace. An important advantage for accountants was the introduction of zero (derived from Arabic *çifr*, 'void'), which was the basis of a radically different and more effective kind of arithmetic. Traditional medieval methods in arithmetic and accountancy (based upon Roman numerals) were seldom displaced by algorism (Arabic numerals and decimal computation) before 1600.

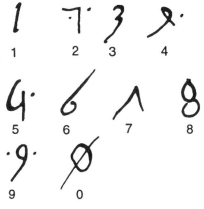

Arabic numerals 1-9 and 0, written in England around 1250.

5
Error and correction

Clerical errors abound throughout the range of formal and informal writing. The medieval scribe spelled words incorrectly and mis-transcribed. He transposed letters, words and whole sentences, confused similar words and substituted erroneously where he misread or misunderstood. He omitted where he should have repeated himself (this mistake is known to palaeographers as **haplography**). He repeated himself where he should not have done so (an error known as **dittography**). Scribal errors may or may not have been noticed at the time of writing, certainly many errors have remained uncorrected. The medieval clerk was, of course, in something of a quandary when he did notice an error because the inks in use at the time were more or less indelible. This difficulty might be compounded if the scribe laboured as a cloistered monk under the strict rule of St Benedict, which frowned upon corrections.

For clerks who were permitted flexibility in making alterations conventional physical and chemical correctives were available. Medieval chemistry offered solutions: recipes developed for erasing text (usually pagan classical writings) from parchments earmarked for reuse. A parchment which was used again after erasure of an original text was known as a **palimpsest** (from Greek words meaning 'to rub smooth once more'). Sometimes the original text can still be made out (with care and the help of an ultra-violet lamp) despite erasure and overwriting – a striking proof of the quality of the original Roman or medieval ink!

The ingredients of the medieval vanishing fluid blended such homely and exotic substances as orange juice, the virtue of nettles gathered in springtime, cheese, milk, vitriol, rock alum and nitric acid. In the absence of these the clerk scratched out his error with a penknife. This practice was allowed even to the four evangelists, who were conventionally depicted as fallible workers, with pen grasped in the right hand and a knife (for correcting mistakes as well as for sharpening the quill pen) in the left hand. The surface of the parchment, roughened by the knife blade, was smoothed with a burnisher of polished agate and restored to writing condition with *pounce* (powdered cuttle-shell) or white paint. The erasure was refilled with revised text or camouflaged with a calligraphic flourish.

Small mistakes might be simply crossed through with an inked line. Correct text might be simply written blackly over the incorrect text. Larger passages were cancelled (from the Latin word *cancelli*, 'lattice') by means of a trellis of inked lines drawn over the offending paragraph. Whole documents were cancelled by a series of herringbone cuts through the centre of the page. Alternatively the clerk wrote the Latin word *vacat* in two halves *va....cat* before and after the text to be deleted. Naturally these disfiguring expedients were not favoured for ceremonious or artistic manuscripts. In these texts the neat clerk might allow incorrect text to stand but would place an unobtrusive dot under the word, letter or minim to be ignored by the reader. This is known by palaeographers as the *punctum delens* ('blotting-out point'). This is an interesting contrast with the modern usage among writers correcting text for the printer: nowadays we put dots under words which we have erroneously crossed out but which we now wish to remain in the text! *Punctum delens* has become *punctum resurgens*!

Words accidentally omitted by the clerk were written in between the lines (**interlined**), their correct position indicated by a **caret mark**. (The word derives from the Latin 'to be in need of'; the sign itself, still in use today, derives from medieval legal shorthand.) More extended insertions were written in a convenient margin, usually preceded by a distinguishing symbol. The place of insertion was indicated by a similar mark above the text. A pair of acute accents stood above words which had been transposed. More serious dislocations were remedied by lettering the offending words and phrases a, b, c and so on in the correct order of reading. The argument (a prefatory outline) to St John's Gospel in the *Book of Kells* (folio 19v) contains a very complicated transposition of text running over some nine lines. The clever clerk, however, retrieved matters by asking the illuminator to indicate the correct order of reading by means of delicate jewel-like signs. Even a mistake was an excuse for embellishment in this most beautiful of books!

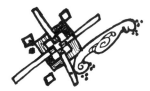

The textual symbol known as 'the turn under the path' marks an Irish scribal error in the 'Book of Kells', around 800.

6
Languages

The languages of Britain are closely related members of a prehistoric family of tongues known as **Indo-European**. The earliest known example of this family of languages was spoken by nomadic tribes who roamed the Caucasus and central Asia before 3000 BC. Their language spread on waves of migration, invasion and cultural interchange across Europe and India. Over the centuries different dialects, and eventually distinct languages (for example Iranian, Hindi, Greek, German, Italian and Irish), developed from the ancestral speech.

The earliest language of significance in the old handwritings of Britain and Ireland is *Celtic*. This was an Indo-European language which emerged during the second millennium BC (perhaps around 1500 BC). One variant of Old Celtic spoken in various dialects across western Europe (including Britain and Ireland) is known as **Q-Celtic** from its characteristic Indo-European **kv** (*qv*) sound, spoken as '**k**' (q, hard c). This is evident in the ordinary word *maq* (Scottish mac) meaning 'son of' or 'descendant of'. Q-Celtic retreated from much of Europe during this first millennium BC and was eventually confined to Ireland. This tongue was spoken by the majority of the people of Ireland down to the nineteenth century. As a written language, **Old Irish** was used by the class of poets and scholars known as sennachies and by the native Christian saints and missionaries who were their cultural successors. Medieval Irish and its modern form (sometimes referred to as Erse by English visitors and commentators) were written down in a wide variety of documents, including personal and business correspondence, diaries, financial accounts and literary compositions. Erse or Irish has survived to the present day as a spoken and written language, boosted since 1893 by the propaganda of the Gaelic League and since 1922 as part of the school curriculum of the Republic.

An early surviving specimen of Old Irish is the writing carved on a memorial stone on Inchagoile, County Galway, which reads: +*lie luguaedon macci menueh*, '+the stone of Lugaed son of Menb'. A rich heritage of Irish writing was assembled by the early Christians of Ireland from the fifth century onwards. This includes chronicles (histories), annals (recording events year by year), law, poetry, lives of native saints, legends of the heroes Cú Chulainn and Mongán mac Fiachnai. Among the early secular manuscripts written entirely in Irish is *Lebor na hUidre* or 'Book of the Dun Cow'. This was compiled before 1106 and contains the legend of *Táin Bó*

Cuailnge ('The Cattle Raid of Cooley'). A further version of this heroic legend was copied into the *Book of Leinster*, which also preserves the earliest personal letter known in Ireland: from Find, Bishop of Kildare, to the scribe Áed Ua Crimthainn. The ancient laws of the Irish were codified in the *Senchas Már* written around 1350. Irish flourished in the hands even of the Norman invaders who, becoming 'more Irish than the Irish', patronised poets and chroniclers bred in the native writing tradition. The *White Earl's Book* was commissioned by James, Earl of Ormond, around 1440 and contains Irish texts and a topography, with genealogy and Irish poetry:

> *A gelgrian forosnai*
> *riched co met noimi*
> *a ri conic aingliu*
> *a choimdiu na nuini na ndaoine*

The lines translate (freely) as a Christian hymn couched in language redolent of the attributes of the pagan god Belenos, 'brilliant fire', and of the Celtic Beltain (May day) festival of fire and light:

> O brilliant sun whose broad beams
> Blaze blessings across the heavens
> O King of all the angels
> O lord of all mankind

The *White Earl's Book* (now in the British Library in London) was given in ransom for Edmund MacRichard (the Earl's nephew) after his capture at the battle of Piltown in 1462.

For occasional translation (of the odd word, phrase or inscription) the palaeographer may solicit the assistance of local members of the Christian Brothers organisation. The basic dictionary is the Royal Irish Academy's *Dictionary of the Irish Language, Based Mainly on Old and Middle Irish Materials* (1913-75) with M. Ó Dónaill (editor), *Foclóir Gaeilge-Béarla* (1977). Guides to learning the language include M. Dillon and D. Ó Cróinín, *Teach Yourself Irish* (1961).

Irish was introduced to north and west Britain during the fifth century AD by Scottish migrants from Ulster, spreading across the highlands and islands and developing into a distinctive language, **Gaelic**, sometimes referred to in old documents as Irish or Erse. Gaelic was spoken widely until the eighteenth century, surviving as the first language of the Hebrides to the end of the twentieth. Gaelic was used for chronicle, poetry, scripture and inspirational literature; for ecclesiastical and estate administration; for secular literature; and for everyday correspondence. The student's dictionary is E. Dwelly, *The Illustrated Gaelic-English Dictionary ... to which is prefixed a concise Gaelic grammar* (1901-11). The recent revival of Gaelic, romantically from Glasgow to Inverness, popularly in the western isles, has stimulated the publication of numerous helpful primers and teach-yourself books. Residential courses in Gaelic language and culture are held at the Gaelic School, Sabhal Mor Ostaig, in Skye. Gaelic in Scotland is the special province of *An Comunn Gaidhealach*, the Gaelic Council formed to promote and preserve the language.

Irish was spoken and written in the Isle of Man from the sixth century AD. This developed into the distinctive Manx dialect which was written from the seventeenth century and spoken until the twentieth in the north of the island. Standard Manx-English dictionaries are A. Cregeen, *Fockleyr ny Gaelgey* (1835, reprinted 1984) and J. Kelly, *Fockleyr Gailckagh as Baarlagh* (1866, 1977).

P-Celtic languages were spoken across western Europe (but not Ireland) from the eighth century BC, characterised by the **p**-sound of certain words, for instance *epos* 'horse' (in place of Indo-European **kv**, qu, in *ekuos*). In British P-Celtic *ap*, 'son of' corresponds to Q-Celtic *maq* (mac); *pen*, 'head', to *ceann* (with hard **c**); *pedwar*, 'four', to *cethir* (with hard **c**). In Wales P-Celtic flourished and was written down, particularly for religious texts such as the eighth- and ninth-century entries (in a spiky minuscule script) in the Latin *Gospels of St Chad* (a manuscript perhaps emanating from southern Wales around 725). A vernacular version of the laws of Hywel Dda was inserted in the *Black Book of Chirk* of around 1190-1250. Welsh verse was preserved in the *Black Book of Carmarthen* (around 1250) and prose in the *White Book of Roderick Mabinogion* (around 1325). From the fourteenth century onwards writings in Welsh included religious and literary prose, poetry, family correspondence, genealogies, annals, monumental inscriptions, estate records, leases, title deeds, wills and legal petitions. Welsh remains a living language, taught in schools down to the present. The standard Welsh dictionary is *Geiriadur Prifysgol Cymru* (from 1950, in progress). English-Welsh/Welsh-English dictionaries for the student include H. M. Evans, *Y Geiriadur Cymraeg Cyfoes* (1981).

Cornish (and its close relative **Breton**), a derivative of British, flourished from the fifth century. By 1700 the language was confined to fishing villages in Cornwall with Breton contacts and died out around 1800, traditionally in the person of Mary Penruffin. For advice and translation, palaeographers approach the Federation of Old Cornwall Societies, Tremarsh, Launceston, publishers of K. George, *The Pronunciation and Spelling of Revived Cornish* (1986) and of the standard dictionary by R. M. Nance, *A New Cornish-English Dictionary* (1938). Courses are offered by the Institutes of Cornish Studies at both the University of Exeter and Redruth

Technical College.

Latin, the language of the Roman administration of southern Britain from the first century AD, was adopted by the medieval church, the law, civil service, the universities, science, manors and business throughout Britain and Ireland. This international language was officially abandoned only in 1733. For translating Latin writings, the most useful dictionary is R. E. Latham, *Revised Medieval Latin Word-list* (1965), underpinned by Lewis and Short's classical *Latin Dictionary* (1879). E. A. Gooder, *Latin for Local History* (1961) is 'a self-teaching manual and guide to the kind of Latin met with in historical records. It had its origin in a course for extramural students of local history who had no Latin themselves, and it is unique in dealing *only* with the Latin encountered in historical documents'.

Norman-French originated among the Norse settlers of northern France (Normandy). The language was introduced to England during the eleventh century (especially after 1066), and to Scotland and Ireland during the twelfth century. Norman-French was spoken in court, castle and church by the Anglo-Norman ruling class (and by their hirelings). It was the written language of romance, jonglery (minstrelsy) and chivalry, and was employed for administrative documents including charters (until the four-teenth century), acts of Parliament (until the fifteenth century) and for the year books (fourteenth-century reports of law cases taken most commonly from the public records). Familiarity with modern French gives a basis for understanding Norman-French writings, with the assistance of R. Kelham's *Dictionary of the Norman or Old French Language* (1779, reprinted 1978). Anglo-Norman vocabulary survives in current use as the jargon of heraldry (the art and science of coats of arms):

The arms of the de Lacy family of Middlingham.

71

> quarterly, 1 and 4, argent on a chevron vert, between
> three wolves passant reguardant sable armed and langued
> gules, as many Lacy knots of the field (for De Lacy);
> 2 and 3, azure, crusily fitchy two dolphins hauriant embowed
> and addorsed or, within a bordure engrailed of the
> second (for Fitzgerald)

'In the first and fourth quarters: silver on a green chevron, between three black wolves, passing and looking sideways, with red claws and tongues, three Lacy knots of silver; in the second and third quarters: blue, scattered with little gold crosses with pointed shafts, two golden dolphins leaping, arching back-to-back, within a golden border of curvilinear indentations'.

Scandinavian (**Norse**) languages were spoken from the eighth century onwards in Yorkshire, Cumbria, the northern and western isles of Scotland, Man and Norse trading posts in Ireland. The dialects of Viking warriors (and of the farmers, merchants and kings who followed them) live on in a multitude of place-names, in charters, in runic inscriptions and in the rich heritage of saga literature. The last Norse dialect surviving in Britain, Shetland Norn, died out during the nineteenth century. The standard dictionary, J. Jakobsen's *Etymological Dictionary of the Norn Language in Shetland* (1928), is supported by E. V. Gordon, *An Introduction to Old Norse* (second edition, 1957).

English, a Low German variant of the Teutonic branch of the Indo-European family, originated among the Angles, Saxons, Jutes and Frisians of the European coasts from Rhine to Skagerrak. Four dialects emerged as settlers spread across post-Roman England: Northumbrian (Anglian), Mercian, Kentish and West Saxon. Known collectively as **Old English** (or Anglo-Saxon) these Germanic tongues were employed as the spoken language of the people and, in formal garb, as the written language of charters, correspondence, chronicles, histories, scripture and literature (sagas, poetry, epics and translations). The palaeographer turns for assistance and instruction to B. Mitchell and F. C. Robinson, *A Guide to Old English* (fourth edition revised with prose and verse texts and glossary, 1986). Sweet's *Anglo-Saxon Reader in Verse and Prose* (numerous editions) is a useful and entertaining adjunct to self-instruction, assisted by selections such as R. Hamer, *A Choice of Anglo-Saxon Verse* (1970). The extensive series of editions published in Old English with translations by the Early English Text Society includes Anglo-Saxon verse riddles. These sound as vigorously, as poetically – and as bawdily – today as when first sung to appreciative warriors such as the eponymous hero Beowulf and King Hrothgar in the great hall of Heorot.

Middle English emerged from Old English during the twelfth century as the spoken and written language of England. Middle English spread thence to the west and north, continuing dominant in England down to about 1500 and in Scotland to 1700. Its vocabulary displays a richness of medieval technical jargon, everyday nouns, verbs and constructions which still endure in dialect speech and writing. Three chief dialects of Middle English (northern, midland, southern) are recognised by linguists: students of old writings immediately distinguish the gruff gutturality of the northern voice from the more lisping numbers of southern England (epitomised by Chaucer). Middle English was employed for most literate purposes including poetry, **hagiography** (writings about a saint's life), homily (sermon), chronicle (a history), biblical translations and exposition as well as charters, wills, business accounts, monumental and other inscriptions.

The palaeographer's **vademecum** (handbook) is *A Middle-English Dictionary* by F. H. Stratman, revised by H. Bradley (1891), with the academic buttress of the *Middle English Dictionary* (University of Michigan, from 1952, in progress). Middle English may be readily self-taught through literary readers such as J. A. W. Bennett and G. V. Smithers, *Early Middle English Verse and Prose* (second edition, 1968), which includes an extensive glossary and grammatical introduction to a confection of chronicle, bestiary (medieval moralising encyclopaedia of animals), fable and biblical commentary.

Modern Scots dialect derives its distinctive vocabulary and pronunciation largely from Middle English. Scots speech contains many anachronisms preserved popularly by rural conservatism, revived romantically by authors such as Burns and Scott, nurtured nationalistically by modern nostalgics such as Hugh MacDiarmid and the Corries and elevated academically in W. A. Craigie, *A Dictionary of the Older Scottish Tongue* (from 1974, in progress), with M. Robinson, *The Concise Scots Dictionary* (1985) as an affordable volume for the palaeographer's bookshelf.

Modern English emerged from Middle English during the late fifteenth century. Old English gutturals vanished from standard English speech, though continuing to bedevil English spelling in words such as cough, thought and borough. Noun plurals simplified, except for the notable man, men; ox, oxen; brother, brethren. Vowels changed pronunciation, though not necessarily spelling. Thus a word such as 'clerk' – pronounced as spelled in medieval times – was transformed in pronunciation to rhyme with 'bark'.

As Renaissance writers introduced new words from Latin and Greek, older English words, despite impeccable pedigrees, were denigrated as the infelicitous (even obscene) slang of knaves, clowns and rude mechanicals. But even modern English, the language of Shakespeare, has power to perplex. The meanings of words shift from generation to generation, technical jargon and fugitive slang shift senses, surface and submerge. The academic might of the *Oxford English Dictionary* is required to wrench an 'original' (say fifteenth-century) meaning even from such homely words as nice, fond, silly, still and sad.

Learning the languages of old writings presents few difficulties. Part-time and evening courses are available, offered by the local education authority or university extramural department. Informal courses may be organised by groups of enthusiasts (such as the local history group), perhaps through the Workers' Educational Association (WEA). Full-time university courses are available in all British languages (living and dead). The ancient forms of British and Irish languages (including English) are readily self-taught for anyone with a firm grasp of the modern tongue and access to a dictionary, a primer and a selection of literary editions. Professional instruction is often available near at hand from teachers of modern language and literature who are generally versed also in older forms and dialects. Help with the odd unfamiliar word (including difficulties with foreign and dead languages) may be obtained from a friendly librarian, teacher, archivist or priest – who may indeed be willing to translate at some length.

A Latin inscription in Lombardic capital letters gave dignity in civic heraldry, as here in the SIGILLVM (document seal) COMVNE (belonging to the community) BVRGENSIV[M] (of burgesses) DE (of) SCARDEBVRG (Scarborough).

7
Dates

The passage of time fascinated the ancients, whose inscriptions and writings remarked, recorded and counted the cycles and epochs of heaven and earth. Priests and witch-doctors regarded the annual cycle of the sun, the seasons and the fixed stars with awe and reverence – learning through close observation that the year extended a fraction over 365 days. In Britain before 3000 BC the farming peoples of the new stone age constructed elaborate chambered tombs for the bones and the spirits of revered tribal ancestors. Some of these tombs were built so that the entrance passage was lighted once a year by the midwinter or midsummer sunshine at sunrise or sunset. Circles and lines of stones were arranged across the countryside and rites were perhaps performed among these standing stones according to a strict astronomical calendar of season, solstice, equinox and eclipse. Prehistoric priests also observed rituals connected with the moon, according to the complex calendar of its mysterious changes: the 29.5 day lunar month from one new moon to the next; the 18.61 year cycle between the events which astronomers now call the major standstills of the moon; and the 19 year jubilee when solar and lunar cycles coincide. Symbolic inscriptions carved on British prehistoric monuments (circular cup-marks, concentric rings and linked spirals) are interpreted by a few prehistorians as the most ancient calendrical notations on earth – perhaps a record of the performance of successive stone-age rites.

Counting the years

The English words 'year', 'day' and 'hour' are all derived ultimately from a very ancient Indo-European word conveying a basic concept of time and its passing, especially in terms of the sun and the gods. The word **calendar** derives from an Indo-European word associated with the idea of 'counting'. Calendrical fashions and methods of counting the years, of course, vary considerably between ages and cultures. The reader of old writings therefore needs to be familiar with a number of dating methods. Although the idea of a calendar is something that humans have struck upon for their own human purposes (whether to predict when the river Nile would flood in ancient Egypt or to fix days for the festivals of the Christian year), it must always be remembered that time is a natural phenomenon. Whatever methods of notation or counting men may devise, time goes on at its own fixed pace. A day on earth is the time taken for the planet to rotate once upon its axis. An earth

75

year is the time taken for the planet to circle the sun. An hour, by contrast, is a unit of time defined by man. An hour might be of almost any duration. A season such as spring has been called an hour. The day has been divided into fractions called hours, though these might be of equal or unequal length according to the fashion of the time or, as one might say, the fashion of the hour!

The various historical methods of counting the years and for organising the annual calendar are described for the palaeographer briefly in C. R. Cheney, *Handbook of Dates* (1945) and at length in N. Harris, *The Chronology of History* (1833). Other valuable additions to the palaeographer's chronology bookshelf are E. B. Fryde, *Handbook of British Chronology* (1986) and A. Dunbar, *Scottish Kings* (1899).

The Jewish people count their years from the era of the creation of the world – reckoned as occurring on 7th October 3761 BC.

Pagan Romans counted their years from the supposed date of the founding of Rome by the legendary Romulus, in the second year of the seventh Greek Olympiad, Roman year 1 (753 BC).

The United Grand Lodge of Freemasons also count from the creation (*Annus Lucis*, 'the year of light') but reckon the beginning of the world to have occurred in 4000 BC.

Archbishop James Ussher (1581-1656) calculated the creation to have occurred in 4004 BC. The Ussher chronology, still accepted by some Christians, is to be seen printed in the margins of the Authorised Version of the Bible.

Christian chronology counts years of grace (as *Anno Domini*, AD, 'in the year of the Lord') from the conventional date of Jesus' birth in the reigns of King Herod and the Emperor Augustus.

An alternative chronological method counted **regnal** years, that is, the years of a prince's reign. Thus the first year of Queen Elizabeth II (written as 1 Elizabeth II) commenced following the death of George VI in the sixteenth year of his reign (16 George VI). Formal documents from the eighth to the tenth century, and from 1189 onwards, were usually dated by regnal year. Regnal years were employed for dating acts of Parliament until 1963. Difficulties arise, however, for the reign of King John, crowned on the movable feast of Ascension Day, whose regnal years are thus of unequal length.

Papal regnal years transcended national boundaries, having relevance throughout western Christendom (except at times when two or three rival popes vied for recognition). English writers might take special pride in the use of papal chronology during the years 1154-9 (1 Adrian IV to 5 Adrian IV), the years of the pontificate of the English cardinal Nicolas Breakspear, known as Pope Adrian IV.

Greek and Roman chronology might, alternatively, reckon in cycles of fifteen years known as **indictions**. These cycles were computed from a first indiction begun in AD 312, on 1st September (for Byzantium) or on 24th September (the Imperial Indiction).

Dividing the year

The pagan Celts of Britain divided their year of 364 days into four equal portions of 91 days. Four chief festivals ensured fertility during the procession of the seasons. *Imbolc* (1st February) was associated with sheep, the lactation of ewes and the fertility goddess Brigid; *Beltain* (1st May) marked the start of open pasturing; *Lugnasad* (1st August) was connected with harvesting crops and the Gaulish god, Lugos. *Samain* (31st October/1st November) marked the end of one pastoral year and the beginning of the next, and the ritual mating of gods and goddesses in a night of spectral terrors whose focus in a devout household was a severed head (or, more recently, a turnip lantern).

These crucial turning-points in the year were absorbed into the Christian calendar. The festival of *Lammas*, 'loaf-mass day' (1st August), celebrated the first bread baked with the newly harvested corn. *Candlemas* (2nd February) retained a fertility element as the feast of the purification of the Blessed Virgin Mary. May Day festivities were not suppressed by the church until the Reformation and were revived, usually under local church patronage, in the nineteenth century. On the night of 31st October/1st November, the eve of the Christian festival of All Hallows (All Saints, popularly known as Halloween) particular devotions were required.

Pagan Celts divided each quarter of the year into a 49 day and a 42 day portion with further subdivisions based upon the magical prime number seven. Several of the Ogham inscriptions of Pictland (which transliterate into no known language) may be read, not as words, but as calendrical memory aids. The characters seem to group in multiples of the calendrical seven.

The seven-day week was observed by the Jews and other eastern peoples as well as by the Celtic and Germanic nations of northern Europe. Germanic deities, gods and goddesses worshipped in England by the Anglo-Saxons, gave names to days of the week: Tuesday (*Tiw*), Wednesday (*Woden*), Thursday (*Thor*) and Friday (*Frigg*).

The words for moon and month in various languages are closely related. The idea behind both words is the measurement of time according to phases of the moon. The Roman year was divided initially into months, beginning with March (named for the god Mars). The original numbering of the Roman months survives in the names of, for example, September (*septem*, 'seven') and December (*decem*, 'ten'). The original fifth and sixth months

(*Quinctilis* and *Sextilis*) were renamed in honour of the Caesars Julius and Augustus (July and August). The twelve Roman months were given 31 and 30 days alternately (January 31, February 30, March 31, April 30, and so on). But Augustus demanded 31 days to equal Julius Caesar's July, so he filched a day from February.

The Roman date was worked out by reference to a day about the middle of each month called *Idus* (Ides), a word associated with the idea of the moon and rekindling of light. The day of the month called *Nonae* (the Nones) fell nine days before the Ides. *Kalendae* (the Kalends) was the first day of the month, a day on which the schedule of religious and political events for the month was proclaimed. (The word Kalends derives from an ancient word for

ROMAN CALENDAR

March

Modern day numbering	Roman date equivalent	Modern day numbering	Roman date equivalent
1	The Kalends of March	16	XVII (17) days before the Kalends of April
2	VI (6) days before the Nones of March	17	XVI (16)
3	V (5)	18	XV (15)
4	IV (4)	19	XIV (14)
5	III (3)	20	XIII (13)
6	the day before the Nones	21	XII (12)
7	The Nones of March	22	XI (11)
8	VIII (8) days before the Ides of March	23	X (10)
9	VII (7)	24	IX (9)
10	VI (6)	25	VIII (8)
11	V (5)	26	VII (7)
12	IV (4)	27	VI (6)
13	III (3)	28	V (5)
14	the day before the Ides	29	IV (4)
15	The Ides of March	30	III (3)
		31	the day before the Kalends of April

'calling out'.) All other days were known as so many days before the Kalends, the Ides or the Nones. This system was adopted by the papacy and by Christian writers generally, declining from common usage at the Reformation, though surviving for Vatican writings until the nineteenth century.

Christian writers might ignore regnal years, Roman months and even the days of the week as they focused upon the mystic chronology of the church. Clerks of the middle ages were clerics, whose spiritual habits spilled freely into their secular writings. Letters and writs were dated according to the feasts and fasts of the Christian calendar: the *octave* of (eight days after) the feast of St Clare the Virgin (19th August); Whitsun (seventh Sunday after Easter); Martinmas (11th November); the vigil of (the day preceding) the feast of St Hugh Aodh Mac Bric of Rahugh (9th November); *Misse domini alleluia* or Quasimodo Sunday (first after Easter). Fairs were named according to the Christian calendar as, for instance, the Lawrence Fair of Forres held from the twelfth century onwards, 'beginning on the vigil of St Lawrence at midday and lasting throughout the eight days next following' (from 9th August until 17th August).

The pivotal episode in Christian chronology was the season of the passion and resurrection of Jesus. Easter, named from *Eostre*, a pagan goddess of fertility honoured at the vernal equinox, was a movable feast. The Christian Eastertide was computed according to strict astronomical criteria which governed the Jewish Passover feast. In Britain, conflicts between clergy inclined towards Rome and priests of the older Celtic church crystallised around the issue of how Easter was reckoned. The matter was settled at the Synod of Whitby in 664, a meeting which marked the beginning of the end for the independence of the Celtic (Irish) church. Easter henceforth was celebrated according to the Roman (English) practice, that is, on the first Sunday after the full moon following the vernal equinox.

Beginning the year

The Venerable Bede employed the year of grace throughout his *Ecclesiastical History of the English People* (compiled around AD 732). Bede began the year on 24th September (the Imperial Indiction). Christian writers began the year at the feast of the incarnation (Christmas). This was fixed on 25th December, falling in with the riotous twelve-day sun-festival known as Roman Saturnalia and also with the north European sun-festival season of Yule. From the late ninth century, as the cult of the Blessed Virgin became popular, Lady Day (the feast of the annunciation), 25th March, was adopted as the first day of the year – though, curiously,

25th March after the nativity was widely preferred: thus *Anno Domini* and the Christian era began not at the conception but three months after Jesus' official birth!

During the sixteenth century various European rulers reinstated the Imperial Roman practice of starting the year on 1st January. (The name January derives from Latin *janus*, 'a door/passage', also from Janus, the two-faced god who looked both forward and backward.) The January date was adopted in Scotland in 1600, but English governments scorned to follow the alien innovation immediately.

Documents written at this time by progressive Englishmen (between 1st January and 24th March each year) were typically given two dates, recognising both English and European practice (for example '22nd January 1592/1593'). England (with Wales and Ireland) finally came into line when the day following 31st December 1751 was decreed to be 1 January 1752.

Calendar reform

Because the earth takes approximately 365.2422 days to make one circuit of the sun, human calendars (which work only in whole numbers) tend over the years to show discrepancies. The fractions accumulate so that after only ten years an error of some 2.5 days is produced. After a mere century or so a full month would separate calendar date (based on a simple 365 day cycle) and the actual position of, say, the midwinter or midsummer sunrise. If left unremedied English Christmas would, after only five hundred years or so, have drifted round to high summer while shivering May Queens would be crowned in November.

This difficulty was appreciated even by the ancients, who periodically reformed and recalibrated their calendars to conform with astronomical reality. Julius Caesar inaugurated a reformed calendar (the **Julian** or **Old Style** calendar), introducing the leap year concept, in 46 BC.

The reformed Julian Calendar remained in general use throughout the middle ages, by which time an accumulated discrepancy of ten days was hard to ignore. And so a new calendar was devised with the assistance of data from the leading astronomers of the day. This **New Style** calendar was indicted by Pope Gregory XIII on 24th February 1582. At first the British rejected this **Gregorian** calendar as a popish innovation. Documents written by British businessmen with European connections, by Roman Catholic priests and by diplomats might be double-dated in Old Style and New Style (OS/NS), for example 31st May/11th June 1590. Britain officially jerked into step with Europe only in 1752, by which time the accumulated error had grown to eleven days. 2nd September was followed by 14th September, and thus the financial year shifted from Lady Day (25th March) to 6th April. Ordinary folk proved more conservative. Even when the calendar riots of 1752 were long forgotten, provincial folk continued to observe Old Christmas in January, as shown by a petition from prisoners in the old tolbooth of Elgin:

> To the honourable Provost of the Brough of Elgan we prisoners humble pitition your honour to give ous somthing to hold our Christmas as it is but very power times with ous at present
> Moray District Record Office, ZBE1 A3/827/1, 3 January 1827

And to this day at Burghead in Moray, a midwinter solstice (sun-festival) bonfire is kindled on 11th January, as a dislocated perpetuation of the Nordic Yuletide revelry.

Ƙt. 1anaıp.   Œnno ᴅomını ᴅccc.° Ł.° uııı.° Suaıplec abbap Œchaıᴅ bo, Œılıll banbaıne abbap Ƀıpop, mael-coba óa Ƒaelan abbap Cluana uaṁa, Ƒaelꞡup abbap Roıp épea, ın pace ᴅopmıepunc. Sloꞡaᴅ mop la hŒm-laıᵬ ⁊ 1map ⁊ Cepƀall ı mıᵬe. Rıꞡᵬal maᵬe Ɵpenn oc paıᵬ Œeᵬo mıc Ƀpıcc, ım maelpecnaıll pıꞡ Ƭeṁpa, ⁊ ım Ƒeꞡna comapba Pacpaıcc, ⁊ ım Suaıplec comapba Ƒınnıo, ıc ᴅenum pıᵬa ⁊ caıncompaıcc pep nƟpenᴅ, coṁᴅ ap ın ᴅaıl pın ᴅupac Cepƀall pı Oppaıꞡı oꞡpeıp pamᵬa Pacpaıc ⁊ a comapba, ⁊ coṁᵬ anᴅ ᴅo ᴅeᵬaıᵬ Oppaıꞡı ı n-ᴅılpı ᴛpı leᵬ Cuınn, ⁊ aᴅpoꞡaıᵬ maelꞡualaı pı muman a ᴅılpı. maelꞡuala pex muman a Ꮋopᴅ-mannıp occıppup epᵬ. Seᴄonnan pılıup Conaınꞡ, pex Caıpꞡı bpaᴄaıᴅe, mopıᴛup.

This is an extract from a chronicle, an annual summary of events considered important by the scribe. This printed edition uses a specially designed typeface that resembles medieval Irish script. Because the cult of the Virgin Mary had not yet been popularised, the scribe counts each year as beginning on 1st January (line 1 'Ianair') rather than Lady Day. Most of the text is in the Irish language. The year is expressed using Latin ordinal numerals: 'Anno domini dccc. °l. ° viii° ('the year of the Lord 800th 50th 8th' – AD 858).

8
Seals and signatures

A written document was long considered a pale shadow of a real deed – a clerical conceit of lesser validity than a physical action performed and attested to by the sworn statements of witnesses who were actually present. Because a piece of writing was less important than a deed actually witnessed, authentication of writings was of little importance. Indeed a documentary record of an event could, without impropriety, be written a day, a month – even a century – after the event narrated. Only gradually did the Latin word *factum*, Norman *fet* and Middle English *dede* (meaning 'deed' in the sense of something physically performed) achieve the meaning **title deed**, in the sense of an accepted evidence of ownership of property in written form.

During the earlier centuries of the middle ages ownership of property was asserted by actual actions with outward and visible signs. Symbolic items were exchanged or exhibited by parties to agreements as a reminder to those who witnessed the act and who might be called upon later to give sworn testimony. A ring was publicly given and received when a contract was solemnised between individuals. A knife or other personal possession was placed upon the high altar of the parish church as a sanctified physical reminder of an agreement or transaction, completed in the sight of God and the congregation.

A solemn dumb-show was played out when taking possession of property. In this procedure, known as **sasine**, the parties were obliged to be present together at the property. 'Seisin' has remained a term for the legal ownership of land. People are still 'seised of' real property. The seller delivered to the buyer a clod of earth symbolising the ground and a piece of wood or a stone symbolising the buildings standing on the property. A handful of corn symbolised church tithes. A small but vital piece of machinery, usually the clapper from the grain-feeding mechanism, symbolised a mill. A single penny symbolised rents due.

Oral testimony by ancient or knowledgeable witnesses and solemn oaths sworn on the sacred relics of martyred saints were sufficient to secure a title to property. Medieval charters therefore included impressive lists of witnesses who, in case of dispute at a later date, would be called upon to swear to what was said and done.

As written evidence came to be acceptable, it became necessary to insure against forgery. Lawyers and administrators devised strategies to ensure that the written document could not be tampered with. It was vital that a document consulted perhaps years after its date of writing could be proved to be the authentic documentary record.

Authentication by **indenture** involved writing an agreement or deed several times on a single membrane, then separating the several texts by means of irregular knife-cuts. One text was retained by each party to the transaction. Any part might subsequently be authenticated by reuniting it with one or other of its companions. For further security, an indented cut might be executed through the word *CHIROGRAPHUM*, 'hand-writing', (or other significant words) written large across the space between texts.

Seals

Medieval European scribes adopted the ancient practice of sealing documents. Monarchs, landowners, businessmen and churchmen chose personal symbols, usually adapted from a coat of arms, as a means of marking documents for the purposes of authentication and security. The owner's sign or device was carved in reverse into a **die** of metal or ivory. This die (or **matrix**) was impressed upon a piece of heat-softened wax or a slug of lead (Latin *bulla* – hence 'papal bulls' for Vatican documents so sealed). Sealing wax was composed of beeswax, strengthened variously with natural resin, pitch, hemp, hair or turpentine. It was most often coloured red, though green, brown and black waxes were by no means uncommon. Shellac replaced wax compounds from the sixteenth century.

The seal could be affixed directly to the surface of a document. This was known by the Norman-French term *en-placard* and was favoured for paper documents. Seals were most commonly moulded on to a tag or cord threaded through and dangling from (*pendant*) the foot of the document. The pendant seal permitted impressions on both the front (*obverse*) and back (*reverse*).

The seal of Isabella, wife of King John. They divorced in 1199.
[SIG]ILLUM ISABEL COMITIS[SE]
[G]LOECESTR[IE ET
M]ORET[VNE:]
'Seal of Isabella, Countess of Gloucester and Mortain'

Seals were generally circular, though women and clerics might affect an elongated (vesica-shaped) seal. Kings depicted themselves enthroned in majesty, armed and mounted. Clerics portrayed their churches, their patron saints and themselves. Landowners favoured heraldic devices. Burgesses, yeomen and even quite lowly peasants possessed seals with devices which might be quasi-heraldic or which incorporated the owner's initials with some commonplace image. Municipal corporations adopted common seals which pictured the battlemented walls of the proudly independent medieval town or perhaps an image of the community's patron saint.

A **legend**, name or title was circumscribed on the seal in appropriate contemporary lettering: *SIGILLVM COMVNE DECRAGFERG*, 'seal of the corporation of Carrickfergus'. Formal Roman capitals were preferred for the earliest seals (up to the twelfth century). A rounded version of the Roman capital, devised in northern Italy and thus known as **Lombardic**, was popular about 1150-1330. This was replaced during the fourteenth century by gothic black-letter inscriptions. Roman capitals returned to favour at the Renaissance. Revived gothic or lower-case lettering gained ground after about 1780.

A seal of around 1180. Willelmus Deo rectore Rex Scottorum: 'William by the direction of God, King of the Scots'.

During the eighteenth century the seal realised a vigorous popularity (though a declining relevance and authority). The gentleman and the businessman acquired a seal matrix in the form of a genteel gemstone, carved with his family crest or personal monogram, to be worn as a piece of jewellery on his watch chain. Similar devices were engraved in gold on a signet ring. These stylish affectations were used to seal the folds on private letters, though seldom for authenticating the most important writings of business, administration and law.

A nineteenth-century variant of the seal habit dispensed with sealing wax. A steel matrix, fixed in an

Embossed seal of Forres Gas Light Company Limited, Morayshire, around 1850.

iron handpress, was applied directly to the written page to raise an indelible embossed device to authenticate the contracts and title deeds of businesses and public institutions.

Signatures

Around 1350 personal subscription became acceptable as a means of authentication. The parties to a contract wrote *words of attestation* – or simply their own names – at the foot of a title deed or across the parchment of a seal tag. Unlettered merchants and craftsmen might draw a simple trade mark, generally a family emblem or a tool of their trade.

The English **scriveners** (copyists of documents) formed a guild to regulate their craft in 1357. In Scotland the copyists were usually trained lawyers, known as **notaries public**. The notaries were authorised to draw up and attest title deeds and contracts of all kinds, recording copies of clients' title deeds in registers known as **protocol books**. These professional writers devised personal marks for attesting the documents they wrote, registered or witnessed. These marks took the form of a complex convolution of calligraphic penmanship incorporating the writer's own name, initials, the sign of the cross and a pithy Latin motto. Scottish notaries' marks were recorded in public registers. English scriveners were registered by the Company of Scriveners of London in formal registers known as the Common Paper.

From the sixteenth century people of all classes attempted some form of **sign manual** (signature) when writing a letter or finalising

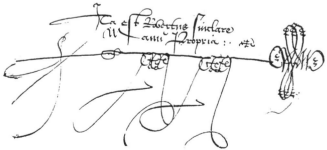

The sign manual of a Scottish lawyer, Robert Sinclair, was used to authenticate his official documents. It reads 'Ita est Robertus Sinclare Manu Propria': 'This is in Robert Sinclair's own hand.'

a deal. Accomplished scribes, graduates of the writing-masters' schools, added elegant humanistic subscriptions to their secretary-script letters. Their names were dignified (and fraudsters deterred)

Signatures of 1705: 'In testimony whereof wee subscrive as follows.
Ja[mes] Chapman   Da[vid] Dalrymple
Ja[mes] Bannerman   Alex[ande]r King
Rob[ert] Bates   Ja[mes] Thomson
*   Hugh Anderson*

by individualising flourishes and joyful excrescences known to palaeographers as **paraphs**. Documents prepared for those who could not write or hold a pen contained a formula such as 'Eduart Hart, John Bairnsfather, Adam Newtoun with our handis at the pen led be the notaris underwretin (at our command) because we can nott writt our selffis'. Thus the dying and the illiterate alike were deemed to have personally subscribed the writing done in their name and at their orders, even though they had just touched the pen while their lawyer did the writing. Other illiterates seized the pen and made what mark they could, perhaps a scratchy shaky initial or monogram. A Christian cross indicated a simple and pious expression of good faith on the part of the unlettered writer, who abdicated responsibility for the actual words written to a lawyer and to the Almighty.

The palaeographer should not assume too much from the evidence of a mere signature. Sometimes, it is true, a shaky signature may provide evidence of illiteracy. But a quavering and blotted mark may just as likely result from haste, a badly made pen, senility or *delirium tremens*. When considering literacy levels among people in the past the palaeographer is ever aware that men and women who saw no pressing need to learn how to write might nevertheless be able to read with fluency. The evidence of a single signature does not prove that the signatory could write anything more than his name. Illiteracy was, in any case, by no means synonymous with stupidity.

An illiterate's mark, 1773: 'Thomas T M Mason his ordinary mark'.

9
Hardware for handwriting

Writers have employed a range of manufactured and natural surfaces for their literary effusions, though numberless texts have vanished as irretrievably as the lessons on a school slate. The quarry workers of Roman Britain carved informal **graffiti** in rustic capitals and cursive script on exposed rock faces. A famous group of runic graffiti was carved on the walls of the stone-age burial chamber at Maes Howe in Orkney, including such gems as 'Ingigerd is the sweetest woman there is ... many a woman has had to lower herself to come in here, despite her airs and graces. Erlingr'. In the parish church bored clerks wiled away the tedious service with a literate penknife. Painted or inked graffiti may occasionally be recovered in the removal of ancient whitewash, wallpaper, paint and plaster.

Potters wrote on the wet clay of their ware: inscriptions on Roman *amphorae* (wine jars) indicate the nature of Britannia's imports (wine, plums, fish sauce, olives, etc). Brick and tilemakers of Rome, too, identified their products with trademarks, names, dates and, occasionally, with more idiosyncratic legends, such as the scrawled boast of a tile-worker at Dover: 'I made 550 box tiles.'

Administrative records of the Roman army, as well as the personal correspondence of individual legionaries, have been recovered in excavations at Vindolanda on Hadrian's Wall. These take the form of thin slats of wood (generally birch or alder) marvellously preserved in the wet earth of the frontier.

Wood was also a favoured material for recording medieval financial transactions. Debts outstanding, money received and commodities delivered were recorded as notches cut on to a wooden tally stick. This baton was then split lengthwise and the two unequal portions (stock and foil) retained by the parties to the transaction. Tally sticks ranged in size from the handy 6 inch (150 mm) slats preserved among Exchequer and manorial records to the ponderous 8 foot (2.4 metre) balk discovered at the Bank of England, recording unredeemed eighteenth-century government debt. The tally stick was inscribed with additional information such as names, dates and details of commodities. These inscriptions were generally in Latin, though Hebrew inscriptions have been noticed; English text is rare. Further explanatory writings were added to labels attached to the parchment filing strips on which the tallies were strung, and to the leathern or stuff bags in which the sticks were stored.

The memorandum pad, sketchbook and jotter of the Roman and medieval clerk alike comprised a pair of wooden boards hinged together. The outer faces were dignified with tooled leather; the inner (working) surfaces were covered with a layer of beeswax upon which the clerk wrote with a pointed metal rod known as a stylus. The wax surface could be written upon, erased, softened, smoothed and reused as often as required. These handy notepads were the subject of one of the riddles of Aldhelm, the seventh-century Abbot of Malmesbury:

Of honey-laden bees I first was born,   [beeswax]
But in the forest grew my outer coat;   [wooden boards]
My tough backs came from shoes.   [leather hinge and covers]
   An iron point
In artful windings cuts a fair design,   [stylus]
And leaves long, twisted furrows,
   like a plough   [lines of writing]

Tablets remained in use throughout the middle ages for copying text, for designing a decorated initial and for planning the layout of a book or charter. To the English of Aldhelm's day the wooden tablet with its waxed writing surface was known by the name *bóc*, hence the modern word book.

Parchment

Parchment, the usual medieval writing material, was prepared from skins of calves, sheep or goats. Skins were used for writing before 2900 BC, but the word 'parchment' is said to derive from Pergamum in Asia Minor (Turkey), a book production centre. The parchment-maker required his skins to come from animals slaughtered by stunning and bleeding so that they would not then be pigmented by blood remaining in blood vessels. For books of the finest quality the clerk required parchment prepared from the soft skins of young, white-fleeced kids and lambs born and killed in the springtime. Acceptable also was skin flayed from unborn calves, which was known as abortive or uterine **vellum**, from the French word *veau* 'calf' or the English 'veal'. Parchments from these sources were thin, smooth and supple, though seldom larger than about 12 by 24 inches (305 by 610 mm). Where a large writing surface was a prime consideration the clerk was obliged to accept the skins of larger, and thus older, animals which yielded a coarser yellowish skin up to 36 inches (914 mm) square.

Converting a newly flayed skin into usable parchment was a complex process. First the skins were soaked in cold running water for several days, then transferred to a solution of lime for a week (or longer in winter). On removal from the lime bath each wet skin was stretched taut on a wooden frame. Here the skin was shorn of remaining hair, scraped free of fat and flesh, then rubbed with chalk, which absorbed excess oils, and allowed to dry. While held in tension on the drying-frame, the skin was shaved to an even thickness with a razor-sharp blade and its surfaces smoothed with pumice and dressed with powdered chalk. Despite this complex preparation the animal origins of the material remain evident in the parchment page. There is a contrast between the smooth white flesh side and the coarser cream-coloured hair side. There are often elliptical holes caused by careless skinning or resulting from wounds and fly bites suffered by the living beast. If a parchment becomes damp, the document curls and cockles – struggling to reassume the shape of the animal originally covered. Having regard for its organic origin, a skin of parchment is usually referred to by palaeographers as a **membrane**.

Paper

Paper was a Chinese invention, probably of around AD 150, which entered the Islamic world by way of Samarkand. Paper reached Europe during the thirteenth century in the baggage of returning crusaders, pilgrims and merchant adventurers. The new material was tentatively adopted for humbler writings during the thirteenth century but did not come into general use until the fifteenth. From the sixteenth century onwards paper began to supplant parchment, being convenient for the writings of businessmen, estate managers and public (especially local government) officials. Paper was particularly suited to the needs of printers.

Paper was manufactured in England from the fifteenth century. In 1490 the craft of papermaking was practised by Master John Tate at Hereford. Most of the paper consumed in Britain, though, was imported, chiefly from France and the Netherlands.

Paper was prepared from linen fibre. The chief raw material was worn-out shirts, sheets and so on collected by rag merchants. The rags were received at the paper works and sorted by hand according to colour, fineness and condition. Batches of rags were then steeped and boiled in a detergent lye, washed clean and bleached in the sunshine (a process known as buckling). After sixteen separate bucklings the rags were marinated in sour milk. The rags were then fermented for two or three weeks (a process known as retting). The retted rags were then cut into 2 inch (50 mm) squares, mixed with water and reduced to a consistent gruel in a mechanical stamping mill. The papermaker then lifted a measure of the mixture in a rectangular sieve (known as a mould). As the water drained away through the mesh, the papermaker's deft manipulation of the mould knitted the fibres of the pulp into a strong web. The sheet of paper pulp was turned out on to a felt mat. This was covered with a second felt and the process repeated until a substantial pile of pulp sandwiches formed. The whole pile was then squeezed in a press to expel excess water. The felts were then removed and the damp sheets of paper pressed again and hung up to dry. At this stage in the process the paper was of a quality something like blotting paper. To make the sheet less porous and to give the sheet its satisfying 'rattle', the limp paper was stiffened with animal **size** prepared from boiled-down bones, horns, hoofs and parchment scraps supplied by the same rag and bone merchants who collected the rags. The sized paper was pressed again, dried and, if appropriate, glazed.

The dry paper retained an impression of the mould mesh as a pattern of translucent lines. When held up to the light, these lines become clearly visible: parallel lines about 1 inch (25 mm) apart, perpendicular to a background of close-set lines (perhaps twenty to the inch). Paper with these characteristic lines is known as **laid** paper. From the eighteenth century a homogeneous mould-mesh left no such marks. This kind of paper is known as **wove** paper. Hand-made papers were not usually trimmed, each sheet exhibiting its craftsmanlike quality with a ragged **deckle-edge**. European manufacturers contrived a wired device in the mesh of the mould. This might be a monogram, a date or a logo,

Animal motif watermark of 1594.

which became imprinted into the manufactured sheet as a **watermark**. Early watermarks have been catalogued for the palaeographer by C. M. Briquet in *Les Filigranes* (1907). Watermarks are useful for identifying a place and date of manufacture as well as the name of the papermaker. One very common watermark image was the head of a jester or fool wearing his distinctive cap and bells. This fool's-cap image gave its name to a standard size of paper (around 16¼ by 13 inches) known as **foolscap**.

Watermark with papermaker's initials of 1664.

The fool's-cap watermark, 1673.

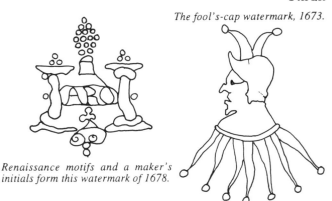

Renaissance motifs and a maker's initials form this watermark of 1678.

Papermaking was mechanised (using French technology) from 1799 onwards. Machine-made paper was produced in a continuous process, the pulp lifted on an endless belt, mechanically shaken, dried between heated rollers and rolled for storage. The rolls were guillotined into sheets for sale, but individual leaves still betrayed their mechanical origin in the microscopic structure of fibres, aligned like logs in a river, along the long axis of the roll. This structure imparted a grain to the sheet, the page folding more easily along the fibres than across, incidentally improving the handling qualities of bound books. Industrial papermakers experimented with alternatives to linen fibre, bulking out the pulp with wool and cotton, flirting with banana fibre, esparto grass, dung, fur, leaves, peat, straw and seaweed. From the 1840s wood pulp reigned supreme. Mechanically shredded, chemically digested, chlorine-bleached wood-pulp paper supplied the immediate needs of mass markets, leaving posterity to discover with dismay that this paper discolours and degrades rapidly (and sometimes irretrievably) under normal conditions of storage and use.

Pens

The word pen derives from the Latin word *penna,* which means 'wing'. The medieval pen was cut from the central hollow rib (quill) of a feather. The natural curve of a quill from a left wing fitted neatly to the fingers of a right-handed clerk. The primary flight feathers of a goose or swan (latterly turkey) were usually favoured, though for fine work a smaller duck or crow quill might be preferred. Fresh quills were allowed to dry and harden over a period of six months or more. Using a small razor-sharp penknife, the clerk first trimmed a feather to a convenient length of about 8

Eadwine of Canterbury, 'prince of writers' (about 1140), shown holding the tools of his trade: a pen and penknife. The open book is artistic licence – books were usually written on loose leaves and bound later.

inches (200 mm), then stripped the feathery barbs from the quill. (The fanciful plumes popularly represented as quill pens are a Hollywood conceit.) The tip of the quill was cut obliquely and the pith-like centre removed. The writing nib was formed by a second oblique cut and by careful trimming of the tapering point. The nib was then slit lengthwise and cut off straight, either at a right-angle to the slit or obliquely, according to the writing fashion of the time. The manufacture and maintenance of pens was the responsibility of the individual writer, a manual skill which some never fully mastered – hence the apologetic punning postscript to many a blotted ink-spattered letter: 'excuse haste and bad pen as the pig

The penknife .... and the correct pen angle. The numbers relate to the writing master's precise instructions for the position of every finger and the angle of the hand necessary for correct writing.

said as he ran up the street'. Quills remained an element in the law stationer's stock-in-trade into the twentieth century.

Experimental pens employing tortoiseshell, jewel-tipped quills and gold nibs were tried by a wealthy minority of writers. Steel pen nibs were manufactured from the 1750s onwards, though only after 1820, with the introduction of mass-production techniques, did cheap, durable and reliable nibs appear on the market. Steel nibs were suitable for the smooth surface of machine-made paper and for the thin inks of the 1830s.

The medieval illuminator outlined his designs with a pointed piece of lead clasped in a wooden handle. The manuscript then passed to the monastic *limner* (painter) whose fine pencil (Latin *pencillus*, 'paint-brush') added the specified colours. The graphite (plumbago, black-lead) pencil was widely adopted from the six-teenth century onwards, though the familiar pencil comprising a graphite core encased in wood was not described until 1683 when the metallurgist Sir John Pettus referred to: 'Black Lead ... curi-ously formed into cases of Deal or Cedar, and so sold as dry Pencils'. The pencil industry proper was created through the genius of the London artist-author-chemist-physicist (and founder of the Royal Geographical Society) William Brockedon. Brockedon patented a method of reconstituting powdered graphite under pressure to form pencil leads of consistent quality. The invention was taken up by Keswick entrepreneurs after Brockedon's death in 1854.

Ink

The word ink derives from classical Greek and Latin words meaning 'burnt-in'. Among the ancients, writing fluids were manufactured from natural substances. These chemically burned into the papyrus or parchment to which they were applied, making a more or less permanent mark. Roman emperors commissioned special ink in the imperial purple colour for their own signatures. This was known by the name *encaustum*. From this word derived the medieval English word *enke* (modern form 'ink').

Ancient inks were blue-black decoctions of natural substances coloured with soot. **Carbon** ink was a suspension of lampblack (from burned animal oils) or charcoal black (from burned vegetable matter, specifically beech wood or peach stones) in an aqueous medium of vegetable gum or animal size. On the Roman documents from Vindolanda messages written in black carbon ink with a reed pen are legible to the naked eye even after being buried for seventeen centuries, though more usually the writing may be read only with the aid of infra-red photography. Carbon inks, however, were only as permanent as the gums which fixed the pigment to the page and were thus always in danger from water, which might dissolve the glue base, and from accidental abrasion, which might scrape the writing from the surface.

Iron-tannin ink was more permanent. This ink was acidic, biting deeply into parchment, indelibly into paper, and mellowing over the centuries to a pleasing rust-brown colour. Medieval recipes for this classic ink required oak galls and iron salts (ferrous sulphate), fortified variously with beer, blood, wine and urine, thickened with vegetable gum (such as gum arabic) and coloured with lampblack.

Unfortunately, traditional acidic inks corroded, and carbon inks clogged, the steel nibs of the nineteenth century. Science came to the rescue of pen manufacturers, inventing chemical writing fluids for a technological age. The carbonaceous inks in black, dark-blue, light-blue and brilliant-red sold by Messrs Stephens were among the most popular. Synthetic aniline dyes (discovered in 1856) were applied to the manufacture of non-corrosive, free-running inks for steel nibs and fountain pens. Experience, however, has proved these products of scientific chemistry less fast and more fugitive (that is, more likely to run or fade) than the homely concoctions of the middle ages.

Palaeographers resort to scientific stratagem for reading faded writing. An older practice involved the application of chemical solutions (ammonium sulphide, gallic acid, etc) to the faded page. These reagents temporarily enhanced the writing but, within a few years, reacted with the ancient paper to leave a uniform, irremediable illegible blackness. Nowadays an ultra-violet lamp (available in libraries and record offices) causes paper to fluoresce and even the faintest of ink to appear black and legible.

The medieval clerk cut and held his quill pen so as to produce a pleasing difference between the thickness of up and down strokes, here exemplified in a feudal property survey from thirteenth-century Northamptonshire.

10
Leaves and gatherings

A single leaf of parchment or paper is the most common form of document encountered by the palaeographer. The word 'leaf' expresses the wonder with which Anglo-Saxons regarded the single pieces of writing material. These supple and slender items recalled the shimmering leaves of the trees. Latin writers expressed the same idea with the word *folium* which means 'the leaf of a tree'. A leaf has, of course, two sides. To the palaeographer the front page of a leaf of parchment or paper is the **obverse**; the back page is the **reverse**. The size of a leaf did not necessarily relate to the document's purpose, importance or origin. Indeed, even a royal charter granting extensive lands to an abbey or privileges to a borough might be succinctly worded and neatly fitted on to a mere 2 inch (50 mm) offcut of vellum.

On the whole, when using parchment, the scribe wrote across the long axis of the membrane. When using paper, the scribe conventionally wrote across the short axis of the page. Vouchers and receipts from the sixteenth century onwards were written across the short axis of paper, which was, however, cut into four or more pieces, resulting in documents about 8 inches (200 mm) across the top and 3 inches (76 mm) down. These slim documents were ancestors of the modern cheque.

For a variety of practical and legal reasons scribes have always preferred to write on just one side of their parchment or paper. A royal charter, especially if embellished with the coloured drawing of the monarch enthroned in majesty, would be displayed in all its one-sided magnificence. Nothing of significance should thus be permitted on the reverse. Paper was usually so thin that the ink showed through to the reverse, making further writing on that side impractical. Scribes writing on a parchment used the whiter, flesh side of the membrane for the text. The membrane's hair-side *dorse* (from the Latin word *dorsum*, 'back') might be employed to carry certain supplementary messages, such as a summary of the contents to assist the filing clerk. These additions were known as **endorsements**.

Personal correspondence, too, was usually written on one side of the paper only. The page was folded, the plain side forming the outside of the package to be sealed with wax or adhesive wafer and to be endorsed with an address. To save postage, correspondents crossed their letters, writing first from left to right then, turning the paper, from top to bottom of the page. This formed a web of interwoven writing. After 1840 this practice declined with postal reform and the widespread use of the envelope.

Rolls

The parchment rolls of the king's chancellor, who also had the title of 'Master of the Rolls', contained office copies of documents sent out with the Great Seal of the realm attached. Chancery rolls typically extended up to 100 feet (30 metres) in length, comprising over fifty membranes sewn head to foot. The main text was inscribed on the flesh-side inner face. On the hair-side dorse, Chancery clerks would, for a consideration, enrol the deeds and wills of private individuals. The dignity of the traditional roll was preserved, in paper, into the seventeenth century by glueing several sheets together in a continuous strip. The courts of common law and Exchequer constructed their record rolls by securing a heap of membranes by cords at their head, then rolling the whole bundle. This practice was emulated for the paperwork of county justices of the peace in their courts of quarter sessions.

Files

Individual papers preserved for future reference could be strung together on a thread or wire. The Latin word for 'string' or 'thread' is *filum*, hence the term 'file' for this method of document storage. Pepys in 1666 referred to his weeding out of 'letters which I have had upon my file for four or five years'. An alternative filing system, employed from the sixteenth century to the nineteenth, involved folding the papers into slim rectangles, endorsing each item with a date and a note of the contents, then tying them as compact bundles for permanent preservation. From the 1840s onwards, civil servants at the Admiralty and Audit Office stored incoming letters flat in bundles of five hundred each, with mill-boards at top and bottom and a good strap to keep them together. As flat filing found favour, inventors swamped the stationery market with a plethora of patent binders, folders and file covers.

Codex

Codex is a Latin word for the familiar bound book. The original meaning of the word was 'tree-trunk'! The Romans wrote much of their day to day correspondence and financial accounts on slender slivers of wood. These were piled flat and strung together for storage. In course of time everyday records were compiled on pieces of parchment, papyrus or paper which were similarly piled flat and bound or strung together for storage.

In the middle ages the codex was preferred to the roll for religious writings (psalters, gospels, homilies, etc) and administrative records (cartularies, parish registers, bishops' account books etc). One was made, essentially, by taking sheets of paper or parchment, say four or eight, folding them in half and stitching them together through the fold. The little booklet thus created is known as a **gathering**. Membranes for decorative texts were carefully arranged in their gatherings to avoid jarring juxtapositions of shade and texture. Wherever the book opened, the reader enjoyed a pair of matched hair- or flesh-side pages.

A gathering may also be created by folding one standard sheet of paper or parchment once, twice, three times and so on, depending on the size of page required. A sheet folded just once into two leaves created four large-size pages known as **folio**. A sheet folded twice, that is folded into quarters (four leaves), made eight **quarto** size pages. A sheet folded three times into eight leaves made sixteen **octavo** size pages. The folded document was then stitched at the centre and the edges cut to create the booklet-size gathering.

For the purposes of ordinary office business the gathering itself (without any binding) was adequate. Much documentary evidence was lost in this way because gatherings (particularly of paper) soon became damaged, dusty and damp. In such condition gatherings were not highly regarded. The Presbyterian church authorities in 1702 found the records of Rothes parish in Moray, in a deplorable state, just loose gatherings. The presbytery of Elgin was thus given a pretext for irritating the godly but troublesome minister of Rothes, Mr James Allan:

> The session minutes of Rothes being return'd,
> And the presbytery finding them only to be some
> stitched sheets of paper, the presbytery did not
> approve of the same, and recommends to the minister
> to have a formally bound book.

When a heap of gatherings was ready the scribe passed the collection to be bound into a codex or book. The binder put the gatherings into a sewing frame and stitched the piles together. The bundle was then **cased** between protective covers or **boards**.

For the most prestigious medieval books, stout wooden boards protected the text. The boards might be covered with embossed leather. The embossed patterns, known as **tooling**, were raised with a range of special tools by skilled craftsmen in the appropriate contemporary style. The boards of a special book might be further glorified by means of pictorial plaques of ivory, silver or gilded bronze set with coloured enamel, crystal and semiprecious stones.

Parchment-covered boards were favoured from around 1600. Some early bindings offer much palaeographic interest when they are stiffened and reinforced with redundant medieval charters, missals pillaged from monastic libraries, paper scrap, etc. A protocol book (a local lawyer's register of deeds and contracts) of about 1610, recently dismantled for conservation, yielded a packing of religious verse in the handwriting of the Scots Renaissance poet, John Guidbrand of Banffshire:

Known as the St John Crucifixion Plaque, this cast metal ornament was made to be fixed to the top board of a seventh-century Irish gospel book.

Johne guidbrand in my hand:
Mark weill my scripture and my law
quhair in than thou sall find
That with my fat I mak a wow
An knits it with ane knot
the treuth it is I luf the weill
be war I hait the nocht

In modern English, this dialect verse reads:
Mark well my scripture and my law
Wherein, then, you shall find

> That with my faith I make a vow
> And knits it with one knot;
> The truth it is I love you well,
> Beware I hate you not

Russia leather was a particularly durable material, favoured by book-binders from the seventeenth century onwards. This leather owed its suppleness and strength to impregnation with oils distilled from birch bark. Russia leather, manufactured from calf, sheep or goat skin, was generally dyed a rich red colour. Green parchment covers were a conspicuous vogue between 1750 and 1830. Full leather binding was usually of calf or goat skin, generally coloured brown or red. The best leather originated in Morocco, a fine pebble-grained material from the skins of goats tanned in a preparation from the sumac shrub. Functional bindings from around 1780 onwards were protected with boards covered in cloth or marbled paper, perhaps with corners and spine of leather. Buckram was a common bookbinding material. This was a stiff durable cotton fabric, said to originate in the manufacturing city of Bukhara in Uzbekistan. Gold-leaf lettering was preferred for the spine if affordable. Ornamental tooling remained a popular feature of the leather-bound book.

Useful to the historian and palaeographer are **endpapers**. An endpaper is a sheet of paper folded to form two leaves. One leaf is pasted flat under each cover of a book, the other forming a flyleaf. A flyleaf is the normally blank leaf which used to be found at the front and back of a book. However, people have always written on these leaves, perhaps details of family births, deaths or marriages, perhaps comments on the text itself, perhaps the summary of a story or some local history.

Some scribes were commonly in the habit of numbering only the leaves rather than the pages of a book. Each leaf has two sides and thus forms two pages, which then have the same number, say 99. The front page of leaf 99 is known to palaeographers as the **recto** (from a Latin term meaning the 'upper or top side') and the back page as the **verso** (from a Latin word meaning 'to turn'). The two pages are thus numbered in old manuscript books as 99r and 99v (or more likely in Roman numerals as xcixr and xcixv.)

From the sixteenth century ready-made books of blank pages could be purchased from the stationers. These books had pages printed with horizontal lines on which to write or vertical lines forming columns for the keeping of accounts. Blank books came in a choice of bindings, ready-labelled account books, minute (written record of meetings) books, registers, and so on. Copies of office letters were made by an ingenious wet copy process on blank tissue-paper pages bound in book form. To produce a copy on a page a letter was placed beneath it, damped with a pad and pressed with a hand press. **Letter-books** are among the most informative of archives.

11
Diplomatic

The study of historical documents is usually known as the art (or science) of **diplomatic**.

In the Roman empire any official written privilege or concession which, for privacy, was folded double was known as a *diploma*, literally a 'double-folded item'. In medieval Europe a double-folded letter was a usual means of communication among cities, bishops and monarchs through the mediation of ambassadors – hence the terms diplomat and diplomacy for the profession of foreign service.

In the context of old handwriting, the study of diplomatic was initiated by Jean Mabillon (1623-1707), a Benedictine monk of St Maur. In his book *De Re Diplomatica* (1681), Mabillon set out to defend various diplomas of the royal French (Merovingian) court whose authenticity had been questioned by a rival (Jesuit) scholar. Mabillon considered each document from a variety of angles (writing material, seal, signature, style of address, names of witnesses, language, place-names, format, etc). His methods were exacting and revealed a high proportion of forgeries among the Merovingian diplomas.

In England the diploma was normally a royal charter. The Anglo-Saxon diploma was a rambling document describing the transfer of land, hence the alternative name of *landboc*, 'landbook'. The document attempted to put down the day's activities in a more or less permanent form and in religious terms, beginning with a preamble on the brevity of man's life and the fallibility of his memory. The wording included horrible curses directed at anybody who might at any time in the future pervert the diploma's intention: witnesses to a transfer of land were not immortal and might not long survive to tell the tale. The document was dated in a wordy elaborate way and instructions on the transfer of property were very detailed. It was supposedly made on the day in front of significant witnesses, including the king, bishop, earl or landowner but was usually written out by the recipient of the property himself (normally a church official). In practice, the witnesses never saw the document. Against each of their names (they did not, of course, sign) was placed the sign of the cross. God would guarantee authenticity.

It was evident to scholars that many diplomas were suspect. During the 1690s George Hickes, Bishop of Thetford, studied critically Anglo-Saxon charters and proved that many were spurious, indeed forged after the Norman conquest on behalf of abbeys and cathedrals. Hickes's pupil, Humfrey Wanley, librarian at the Bodleian Library in Oxford, contributed a critical catalogue of Anglo-Saxon manuscripts to the bishop's treatise (1703-5) on old northern European languages.

The study of old handwriting, though just one element in the investigation of authenticity, was crucial in the final decision. It was therefore necessary to be able to read and identify the normal handwriting of each country, region, century or profession. Palaeography as an academic discipline took off!

Palaeography handbooks appeared from the eighteenth century onwards, notably A. Wright's *Court Hand Restored* (1776). Learned societies were established to pool the scholarly resources of palaeographers throughout Britain, for instance, the now defunct Palaeographical Society (1873-95) and New Palaeographical Society (1903-30), whose publications are required reading.

Diplomatists appreciated at once the crucial significance of handwriting, discovering that an undated document might be datable to within a generation from the evidence of the script alone. Scholars found that affectations and eccentricities in the handwriting might reveal the authorship of anonymous writings, declaring, if not the clerk's name, then certainly his official capacity, educational background, regional origin, beliefs and attitudes to office. This is a form of **graphology**, analysing personality from handwriting. Diplomatists took a fresh look at the clerical output of the middle ages, and especially at the charters which had established the Christian church in its extensive territories and privileges. Canterbury was particularly well endowed through dubious documentation. Researchers discovered a welter of documentary dubieties: documents innocently restored, subtly improved, questionably copied and downright fraudulent. A certain monk named Guerno, a famous medieval improver of **muniments** (title deeds relating to landed estates), confessed on his deathbed to forging numerous privileges on behalf of the claim of the province of Canterbury to be superior to York. Guerno was well aware that for centuries monks (and nuns) had miraculously discovered sacred relics of saints and even of the holy cross on which Jesus was crucified. Nails from the cross were frequently coming to the surface. It was believed that Jesus himself wished these relics to be found to inspire the faithful.

In the realm of charters, Osbert of Clare, who flourished around 1130, was identified as the godfather of a forgery factory founded in the writers' workshop of Westminster Abbey, where Osbert was prior. Osbert's team realised on parchment the oral donations of the benefactors of an earlier unlettered age. Osbert was, indeed, a realist, it might justly be said. He was aware that monarchs and landowners had, for over five centuries, donated thousands of acres of valuable real estate to local churches, monasteries and cathedrals up and down the country. Most of the gifts had been by word of mouth. Diplomas and charters were not at all usual even in Osbert's day. So Osbert felt duty bound to repair the omissions of his predecessors by at last writing down in a charter the various gifts, particularly to Westminster Abbey. Of course the terms of many gifts were reappraised in view of the changing circumstances. As the charters flowed thick and fast from the fertile quills of Osbert's team, vague gifts at last were 'realised', made real. Valuable benefactions were recorded for posterity. The whole of the heavenly host could not but approve this worthy realisation. King Edward the Confessor, particularly, would have been glad to see so many of his gifts to the abbey now recorded in proper (twelfth-century!) charters. In any case he might have preferred the measured clarity of twelfth-century forms of charters to any of the vaguely remembered oral donations and ponderous rambling diplomas of earlier days.

One particular concern of Edward the Confessor had been to remove coronations of English kings to Westminster from Winchester, Canterbury, St Paul's, Kingston-upon-Thames or wherever the particular king thought fit. Edward chose the Saxon minster (and as penance for not making pilgrimage to Rome, reconstructed it) because it had supposedly been miraculously consecrated during the seventh century by St Peter himself. Though Norman kings were, for propaganda purposes, crowned at Westminster, it was later embellishment of the legend and fabrication of evidence by the monks that fixed coronations (as if of immemorial antiquity) at Westminster.

Diplomatic and palaeographic techniques may also be applied to modern documents. The notorious Zinoviev letter of 1924 was concocted to confirm the belief that British socialists acted under Russian Bolshevik direction. The letter achieved its purpose: the Labour government fell. Diplomatic test proved too late that the document was fraudulent.

12
Reading the writing

To learn to read the handwriting of old documents in general, it is necessary to choose just one to start on. This should be a document that is, in the main, readable but with sufficient undeciphered words or letters to provide a challenge. It could be a nineteenth-century letter in the family archives or a photocopy from an eighteenth-century church register. The local archivist (at the county record office or public library) may be approached to provide a photocopy of a typical document of the century or style required. The document should not be too difficult, nor have too many abbreviations or too much scrawl, nor be in a language unknown to the reader.

The archivist may set the novice palaeographer on the way by helping with the first few words. It is essential to read letter by letter, rather than word by word. This permits the beginner to note the form of each letter and its means of linking with adjoining letters. It will be at this stage that the beginner realises the significance of the descriptions in earlier chapters of this book of the letter-forms of each style of handwriting. It will probably be at this stage, too, that the beginner collects examples of letter-forms printed in text books issued by writing-masters. These are obtainable through the public library.

After reading and writing down the transliteration or transcription of the first word, the beginner surveys the result. Is it a meaningful word? If not, the palaeographer considers whether the word in the document was perhaps spelled in an unfamiliar manner, remembering always that, until the eighteenth century, spellings were far from standardised. Professor Gilbert Murray, writing in *The Spectator* (4th December 1936) referred to King John's spelling *yowzitch*, an acceptable medieval English form for 'usage' though employing not one letter of the conventional modern spelling. The beginner asks whether the transcription represents an abbreviated form of a simple word, an obsolete, idiomatic, slang or dialect word not now in everyday use, or a legal or technical term beyond his ken. Or has the beginner made a blunder? Have *f* and long *s* been confused? Have the minims of *i m n u* been miscounted? (These letters are scarcely distinguishable in some scripts.) Has the beginner mistakenly transliterated letters such as *c* and *t*, *b* and *v*, *p* and *x*, which assume superficially similar forms in some alphabets? With such points in mind, the beginner retransliterates any suspect word, making no assumptions except, perhaps, that the expert medieval scribe is less liable to error than the novice today.

104

Fluency comes with practice on a broad range of documents in a variety of styles. When formal charter hands have been mastered, the beginner progresses to the penmanship of clerks in public office as a preparation for the reading of popular writing in literary manuscripts, in private correspondence and business archives. Transcriptions published as academic texts by the Record Commission and facsimiles illustrating palaeography textbooks or scholarly editions support the beginner's practical exercises, allowing any palaeographic efforts to be checked against the interpretations of experts.

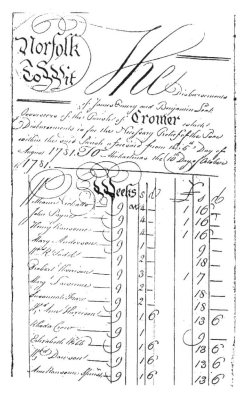

Calligraphic law hand and copperplate demonstrate the penmanship of parish officers of Cromer, Norfolk, in 1781: note the flourishing legalistic W in 'To Wit' and 'Weeks'.

13
Hints for transliteration

Copying the handwriting of an old document by hand is a good way to learn how to read that particular script. Before the days of inexpensive photocopying, the skill of copying was acquired by scribes commissioned to duplicate manuscripts for patrons or employers. Some copyists became so expert that their reproductions could at the time hardly be distinguished from the original document. By this means the medieval copyist, in particular, gained an insight into the varied styles of the past and could write (or forge) any style to order. Legal copyists were renowned for their ability to write – at a price – the peculiar hands of the various courts of law. The palaeographer nowadays may prefer to use tracing paper to follow a scribe's pen across the page. This is what is known as the process of **transcription**: making as exact a copy as possible of the handwriting of the original document. At the end of this process the palaeographer has no more than a reproduction of the original in its original script, colouring and language. But he has an awareness of the manner in which the scribe's hand actually moved across the page, an appreciation of how the letters were formed, a grasp of how the letter-forms of each era evolved from the letter-forms which went before.

Transliteration involves changing an unfamiliar script into a typescript in the normal Roman alphabet. If the script is sixteenth-century secretary hand, each letter is written or typed out in modern form. This incidentally opens up the document to a wider audience, who can read a typescript but not a sixteenth-century manuscript. If the script is cuneiform or hieroglyphic, the symbols are transliterated into the Roman alphabet. This yields a typescript in an unfamiliar language (Mesopotamian, Egyptian, etc).

The document has thus to be **translated** into the language of the modern audience (English, Welsh, Gaelic, etc). This is the third task of the palaeographer.

Occasionally the palaeographer may wish to provide a modern edition and translation of an old document with a view, perhaps, to eventual publication. To make the text accessible to readers, he aims for the most intelligible version consistent with truth to the original. This is a creative process. The sensitive palaeographer strides far beyond the drudgery of dull regurgitation. Palaeography is a realm of revelation which discovers the mind and environment behind the manuscript.

A modern version of an old document must be exact, accurate and comprehensive, preserving the full flavour of the original and each appropriate word, figure, rubric, spelling, capitalisation, paragraph, paraph, italicisation, stop, doodle, insertion, correction and gloss. An edition may reflect the format of the original, its layout, lineation, pagination – even changes of hand, pen and ink. Text lost to mouse gnawings, wormholes, dirt, damp stains, tears and frayed edges may be supplied (if indubitable) within a <diamond bracket> justified by an appropriate footnote. Words, phrases and characters never in the original may be supplied by the editor to assist the reader in [square brackets] in the body of the transcription, or in footnote, appendix and introduction. Manuscripts should not normally be censored.

The palaeographer adopts consistent policies in respect of abbreviations. He may choose to extend without comment; to extend within square brackets; to adopt a conventionalised representation of symbols (in the manner of the Record Commission's record type); or leave matter unextended. The palaeographer's sympathy for the manuscript and for its era will be a guide to the best practice, whether, for instance, to extend a recognised symbol as 'et' or 'and' or '&'; whether *ye*, *q'*, *y'* remain unexpanded or are rendered as the, [th]e, [quha]t, [wha]t, that, [tha]t. The rendering of abbreviations may materially affect sense – and sensibility. Consider for a moment the commonplace abbreviations 'Mr' and 'Mrs'. From the seventeenth century onwards writers used 'Mr' and 'Mrs' in the familiar sense of husband and wife. But 'Mr' at that time might, on the other hand, mean merely that the man was a university graduate, that is a 'M[aste]r of Arts'. 'Mrs' meaning 'M[ist]r[es]s of the household' was also common usage and had no implications concerning the woman's marital status. 'Mrs' also meant 'mistress', meaning an unmarried woman or girl, equivalent to the modern 'Miss', which is itself an abbreviated form of mistress. Finally, of course, a man's 'Mrs' in the pejorative sense 'mistress' certainly was not his spouse! 'Mr' and 'Mrs' in old writings cry out for an footnote explaining the relationships for the reader.

Latin abbreviations may not immediately suggest an extended form. For the common *Habnd et Tenend*, 'to have and to hold', of Latin title deeds editorial practice varies. Essex Record Office has favoured what grammarians term an unattracted gerund *Hab[e]nd[um] et Tenend[um] una[m] bovata[m]*. Other archivists have considered that, for more elegant Latin, the extended words should decline as gerundives agreeing with their nouns: thus *Hab[e]nd[am] et Tenend[am] una[m] hida[m]*, but *Hab[e]nd[as] et Tenend [as] decem acras t[er]rae*.

In the transliteration of initial and capital letters the palaeographer adopts a consistent policy based upon familiarity with medieval practice. Letter form (rather than letter size) usually provides the key. For instance, the thirteenth-century initial *A* and initial *M* may be transliterated as capitals even though neither may have been written larger than *a* or *m*. On the other hand the enlarged initial *c* and initial *s* favoured by some round-hand writers might not require transliteration as capitals despite having been written no smaller than *C* or *S*!

The manuscript under consideration is carefully identified by title, date and provenance, for example: '*The Book of Uí Mhaine* (also known as *Book of the O'Kellys*), Royal Irish Academy Ms. D.ii.I and British Library Ms. Egerton 90, before 1394'.

An extract from an extended archival document is usually identified by provenance, reference, type of document, originating authority, date and page number (specifying recto or verso), thus: 'Moray District Record Office, ZBFo A52/6, register of sasines, Forres burgh, discharge and renunciation of heritable bond, 5 July 1726 (35r - 35v)'.

It may be appropriate to add a description of the manuscript: material, watermarks, ink, page-size, format (including binding style), rulings, seals, indentures, etc.

Palaeographers are keen to share their discoveries and enjoy lively debates with fellow enthusiasts. By pooling palaeographical skills, transliterations are improved and refined. Outstanding difficulties may be resolved when a fresh eye is brought to bear. Expert linguists help to hone a translation from a stilted gloss into good English appropriate to the content of the original. Academic historians explain the meaning of transcribed texts – their historical, philosophical and bibliographical significance. The palaeographer acknowledges debts to the expertise of colleagues. In preparing the following examples, our circle of correspondents has included: Michelle P. Brown, British Library; D. J. Butler, Durham County Archivist; David Clement, Sgoil Eolail na h-Alba, Edinburgh; P. W. Davies, National Library of Wales; David d'Avray, University College London; Eurlys Gallagher, Walters Ash, High Wycombe; Vic Gray, Essex County Archivist; Diana Greenway, Institute of Historical Research, University of London; Vivien Hamilton, The Burrell Collection, Glasgow; B. C. Barker-Benfield, Bodleian Library, Oxford; Mrs Neli Jones, Pontrhydfendigaid; Miss J. M. Kennedy, Norfolk County Archivist; Leslie Macfarlane, King's College, Aberdeen; Malcolm Parkes, Keble College, Oxford; Derryan Paul, College of Librarianship, Aberystwyth; Miss Lorna Pike, Dictionary of the Older Scottish Tongue; Grant G. Simpson, King's College, Aberdeen; H. D. Watson, Dictionary of the Older Scottish Tongue; Edward Weiner, Oxford English Dictionary; David Weston, Glasgow University Library; Miss E. D. Yeo, National Library of Scotland; and, for bibliographical services, Alwyne Slasor, Culloden.

14
Specimen texts

The eighteen documents that follow were written between the years 690 and 1883 and are of different types (religious, scientific, administrative, legal and personal). In order to encourage the beginner in palaeography, and to get the general reader started, we have explained at some length the first four of these texts and have provided background information to each – their scripts, languages and historical circumstances. Then we show how to decipher a key portion of the text, in the proper, careful, palaeographical fashion, letter by letter, word by word.

The other thirteen are presented as palaeographical exercises set out as the palaeographer would expect to find in a published edition. The texts are interpreted through an introduction, a transliteration and, as appropriate, a translation. Notes draw attention to matters of special significance.

The reader will probably wish to try and work out experimental transliterations and/or translations unaided, though in case of difficulty our transliterations may prove useful as an occasional crib.

The examples are graded by degree of difficulty using the rock-climber's classification:

moderate	*
difficult	**
very difficult	***
severe	****
very severe	*****

The beginner is, perhaps, advised to resist the five-star challenges until some of the two- and three-star obstacles have been surmounted.

I GOSPEL BOOK 690 and 980
****

The *Lindisfarne Gospels* were written out in the monastery of Lindisfarne, Northumbria, under the direction of Bishop Eadfrith around about the year 690. The gospels are those of the New Testament saints Matthew, Mark, Luke and John. The version of the gospels then in use was that of the fourth-century St Jerome, written in Latin. At Lindisfarne the gospels were gorgeously illuminated by expert scribes and artists in honour of the local Anglian saint Cuthbert. In artistic terms the manuscript is in Celtic style. Lindisfarne was originally settled by Christians from Celtic Ireland.

A letter in Latin on parchment explaining the canon table to the Lindisfarne Gospels, 690 AD, with a later Old English translation interpolated.

The *Lindisfarne Gospels* were written on parchment pages and bound to form an impressive book of folio size. The original **gospel book** survived the raids of Norse pirates and the harrowing of northern England by William the Conqueror. The volume even survived the destruction of medieval texts at the Reformation to be rescued by antiquarian collectors of historical documents. As one item in the extensive accumulations of the Cotton family, the volume was acquired by the new British Museum in London during the eighteenth century as part of a policy to preserve such collections for the nation. The original is now in the British Library under reference Cotton Nero D.iv.

Prefaced to the *Lindisfarne Gospels* is a **canon table**, a system for cross-referencing significant parallel gospel texts. This was devised in the fourth century by Eusebius, Bishop of Caesarea. The system is explained in a letter to a Christian named Carpianus, the beginning of which forms the text here quoted. The letter refers to previous scholarly endeavours of Ammonius of Alexandria. He had used St Matthew's Gospel as a basis to combine the four gospel texts into a single gospel story. This was known by its Greek title of the *Diatessaron Gospels*, which literally means 'combining four'.

In this extract there are nine lines of Latin text with nine lines of translation into Old English. The larger handwriting is the Latin main text. Its style is peculiar to Britain and Ireland and known as insular half-uncial. It was written around the year 690. The smaller handwriting tucked above the main text, line by line, is in Old English. This is known as a gloss, which is a type of informative translation. It was intended to help those in England who, in the tenth century, were not very familiar with Latin. The handwriting is some three centuries later than the main text. This handwriting is known as insular spiky minuscule. The gloss was provided by a Saxon named Aldred.

The Latin text in large handwriting is on lines 2, 4, 6, 8, 10, 12, 14, 16, 18. The Latin is not much abbreviated. In other words, virtually all the letters of each word have been written out. There are, however, several abbreviated words which we have extended to full length by supplying missing letters. Our additions have been placed within square brackets.

The Latin text (on the left) and the modern English translation (on the right) are as follows:

2	EUSEbius	Eusebius
4	carpiano	to Carpianus
6	fratRi iN d[omi] No Salutem	brother in the Lord, greeting
8	ammoNiuS quidam	A certain Ammonius
10	alexaNdriNuS magno	the Alexandrine with great
12	studio atq[ue] iNdustria	study and industry
14	uNum NobiS pRo quat	one [gospel] to us for four
16	tuor euaNgeliiS dereli	[four] gospels has be queathed
18	quit Namq[ue] trium	[bequeathed] and of the three [gospels] ...

The Old English gloss in spiky minuscule is set out on lines 1, 3, 4, 5, 7, 9, 11, 13, 15, 17. There are a few abbreviations and we have supplied what is missing in square brackets, and substituting 'th' for crossed d and 'w' for *wen*. The English gloss reads:

1	eusebius	Eusebius
3	[th]ecarpian	to Carpianus
4	isca	

5	dæ[m] bro[th]er in drihten haelo	brother in the Lord greeting
7	gelaered sum o[th]er	a certain learned
9	alexandrinesca mi[th] micile	Alexandrine, with great
11	bigeong [and] ec hogahscipe	cultivation and also prudence
13	enne [ue]l án ús fore feo[w]er	one or a single [gospel] to us for four
15	godspellum of forleort	gospels replaced
17	[and] for[th]on [th]rea [ue]l [th]ara gods<pellera>	and therefore of the gospels ...

Proceeding letter by letter, consider, for instance, line 6 (in Latin). The first letter of the first word is a half-way stage between capital *F* and small *f*, with a tag to the left. It is, of course, an **f**. It is joined to the second letter. The second letter resembles a small modern *n*. A letter resembling *n* in this half-uncial script is always an **r**!

The third letter is a small round character like a modern *a* fused to a *c*. It is, in fact, a simple **a.** Next comes a rounded letter with a horizontal cross-stroke on its head. This is **t**. Next appears the capital form of **R.** Lastly there is a straight stroke which could be capital or small **i**. It is undotted but with a serif on its head. There is a slight gap after **i** which happens in this case to indicate the end of the first word. The word is **fratRi**. In Latin this is the dative singular of the ordinary word *frater*, meaning 'brother'. It is dative to agree with the name *Carpiano*, which is also dative, meaning 'to' or 'towards', that is, 'to Carpianus'.

The second word commences with the same letter as at the end of the previous word. It is an **i**. The second letter looks like a square without a top, but is a capital form of **N** (not to be confused with *r* which resembles a modern small *n*). There is no gap after **N**, but here is the end of the Latin word **in** meaning 'in'.

The third word is an abbreviated form. This is evident from the line above the word. Read what is actually in the text before proceeding. First there is a little round letter with a trailing tail to the left. This is a **d.** The second letter was already deciphered in the word *in*. It is a capital **N**. The third and final letter is evidently an **o**. The word is **dno**. In Martin's *Record Interpreter* (page 42) there is a choice of readings for *dno*. There is *domino* meaning 'to the Lord' and also *dono*, 'I give'. Only *domino* makes sense in the sentence.

The next word begins with a capital **S**, then a small **a** (like the *a* in *fratRi*, seemingly fused with a *c*), next a crooked **l** and an obvious **u**, a rounded letter distinguished from square-box **N**. The fifth letter appeared as the fourth in *fratRi*. It is a **t**. Next there is an

112

obvious **e**. It is followed by three minims, which could be *in* or *ni*. Only **m** makes sense here, to complete the Latin word **salutem**, 'greeting'.

Now consider line 13, which is the Old English gloss to the Latin line beginning with *uNum*, 'one'. The first letter in the spiky minuscule Old English text is small **e** with its distinctive crossbar shooting to the right to touch the next letter formed with two minims linked at the top. This is **n**. The next letter (two minims) is **n** again. Then follows another small **e**. The word is **enne**, meaning 'one' and recalling the modern dialect form *ane* still used in Scotland and northern England for 'one'.

The second word has just one letter – a tall single upright stroke with a curved foot and slanting crossbar. It is **l** with a line through to indicate an abbreviation. Martin's *Record Interpreter* (page 79) suggests that this abbreviation stands for the Latin word **vel**, 'or'. The glossator has used a Latin abbreviation for an English word just as we today might do when we use i.e. (Latin *id est*) for the English 'that is'. The beginner may have thought that the crossed *l* looked like a tall *t*. But look at the **t** in **drihten**, 'lord', in line 5, where spiky minuscule **t** is a small letter with no ascender rising above the top stroke.

The next word follows with scarcely a gap. Its first letter is **a** with an acute accent above. Then follows **n** almost, but not quite, linked to the letter before. The word is **án** meaning 'one'. The glossator has provided alternative English forms (literally 'one or one' for the Latin *uNum*.

The fourth word begins with small **u** (two minims more or less linked at the base) with an accent above. In old handwritings *u* is often accented so that the reader cannot confuse its two minims with other minim letters such as *n*. Next comes spiky minuscule **s**, a sort of long *s* with a descender below the line. The word is **ús** as a dative case meaning here 'to us'.

The fifth word begins with **f** descending below the line and with a tag to the left. This letter is quite similar to the **s** which precedes it – only the tag is really different. The tag is the key to differentiating long *s* and *f* in old handwritings. Now, clearly, comes **o**. The third letter splays open and points a leg downward (like a badly penned **n**). This is spiky minuscule **r** which must be carefully observed and distinguised from *s*. The last letter was seen in the first word of the line. It is **e**. The word is **fore** meaning 'for'.

The sixth word begins (like the fifth) with **f**. The **e** and **o** which follow should present no problem. The next letter will not be familiar and just has to be carefully observed and learned. Note the flat-topped bow of the letter and its spiky pointed descender. It is a characteristic Anglo-Saxon letter: not *p*, which is written splayed open (see

[th]ecarpian on line 3); nor is it *thorn* (because our glossator prefers a crossed *d* for *th*). This is Anglo-Saxon *wen* (**w**). The last two letters were in **fore**. They are here the other way round as **er**. The word is **feo[w]er**, meaning 'four'. The Anglo-Saxon spelling hints at the way it was pronounced. Indeed, in Scots and northern English dialect 'four' is still pronounced as though spelled *fower*.

Taken as a whole, this line of text has the cadence of an Old English poem. The Anglo-Saxons delighted in puns and riddling word-play. In song and in spoken verse, alliteration (that is, repetition of similar sounds rather than rhyme) fell pleasurably upon Anglo-Saxon ears. Our glossator was bred in this lyrical poetic tradition. He therefore chose his words very carefully for their sound as well as their sense and allowed himself the extravagance of the alternatives *enne* or *án* to give the line a proper poetic balance. Much early writing (including this text) was intended to be read aloud in a ceremonious manner. To appreciate this, read the line aloud, slowly and with the dignity a church text should deserve. Listen to the poetic sound of the line and enjoy the authentic voice of an English scholar-poet of a thousand years ago. This is a delight of reading old handwriting!

So much, then, for line 6 (Latin) and line 13 (Old English). There are several points worth remarking about the rest of the text. In line 2 the decorated initial word **EUSEbius** is not easy to read because it is written in a manner pleasing to the illuminator's artistic perception rather than the reader's convenience. The artist begins with large uncialised **EU**, then an angular capital **SE**. The last four letters are artistically fitted, **bi** above **us**, at the end of the line corresponding to the upper and lower storeys of the large letter **E**.

In line 3 [**th**]**e** is the dative singular of [th]u and means 'to thee'.

In line 5 the first word illustrates several points. Firstly, the scribe has written **d** when he intended crossed **d**. The omission is serious because 'd' and 'crossed d' were completely different letters representing the d-sound and th-sound respectively. Secondly, we see the common Anglo-Saxon **æ** diphthong, which is quite unlike the separate 'a' and 'e' in **haelo** in the same line. Thirdly, the mark above diphthong **æ** indicates the omission of 'm'. The whole word is [**th**]**æ[m]**, 'to the, to that', showing that **bro[th]er** is in the dative, 'to the brother'. The glossator gives **haelo** for the Latin *salutem*. From this word derives our modern English words 'hale', though we might translate the word in this context literally as 'hello'.

In line 7 the English writer does not use the name Ammonius but glosses him as 'a certain learned man'.

In line 9 the **i** written above **micle** is an inserted correction to make the word **micile** meaning 'great'. This is the same word as the modern Scots dialect words *mickle* and *muckle*, also meaning 'big' or 'large'.

In line 11 the glossator uses the tironian note abbreviation sign for 'and'. The palaeographer might decide to transliterate this symbol as **&.** There is no hard and fast rule so long as the practice chosen is applied consistently.

In line 17 the glossator provides alternative words **[th]rea** and **[th]ara** (crossed **d** stands for *th*). The full word **god**spellera, 'gospels', is not shown in the photograph, but inserted within diamond brackets.

The entire text can now be read, perhaps with the assistance of our transliteration in which odd numbered lines represent the Old English gloss and even numbered lines the Latin original. A translation is as follows:

> Eusebius to Carpianus, brother in the Lord,
> greeting. A certain Ammonius the Alexandrine
> with great study and industry has bequeathed
> to us one [gospel] for four gospels and thus
> of the three gospels ...

The whole document is now set out line by line. The Old English lines are printed in bold type, the Latin in italics:

1. **eusebius**
2. *EUSEbius*
3. **[th]ecarpian**
4. *carpiano* **isca**
5. **dæ[m] bro[th]er in drihten haelo**
6. *fratRi iN d[omi]No Salutem*
7. **gelaered sum o[th]er**
8. *ammoNiuS quidam*
9. **alexandrinesca mi[th] micile**
10. *alexaNdriNuS magno*
11. **bigeong [and] ec hogahscipe**
12. *studio atq[ue] iNdustria*
13. **enne [ue]l án ús fore feo[w]er**
14. *uNum NobiS pRo quat*
15. **godspellum of forleort**
16. *tuor euaNgeliiS dereli*
17. **[and] for[th]on [th]rea [ue]l [th]ara gods<pellera>**
18. *quit Namq[ue] trium*

II HERBAL 1100
***

The **herbal** was an encyclopedia of useful medicinal plants. Each plant was identified by its various names and the herbalist described how each was to be prepared and how administered in a variety of medical conditions. The herbal also enshrined a philosophical purpose. As a celebration of rich variety and mystic unity, the herbal illuminated the complex interrelationship of plant, animal and man in God's creation.

The standard medieval herbalistic text is known as the *Pseudo-Apuleius* (because it was wrongly attributed to the Numidian satirical poet Apuleius Platonicus, born around AD 125). Three basic versions of the work were in existence by about AD 550, though all of these are now lost. However, from these ancestors descended a numerous family of (cumulatively corrupted) copies and editions.

A parchment page from a copy of the standard medieval herbal, Pseudo-Apuleius.

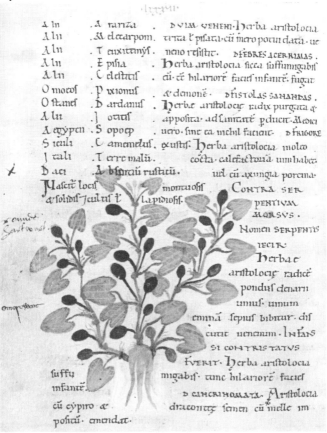

The page illustrated is from a *Pseudo-Apuleius* copied on to parchment by the Benedictine monks of Bury St Edmunds shortly after the Norman Conquest. The Latin syntax of the scribe was, unfortunately, somewhat wanting – and not helped by the garbled original which he had to copy! The modern translator resolves difficulties by turning to alternative texts in other libraries. (There are at least forty versions of the book extant and as many as a dozen in Britain alone.) The translator is also assisted by the compendious edition of the *Pseudo-Apuleius* published in *Corpus Medicorum Latinorum,* volume IV, edited by Ernest Howald and Henry E. Sigerist (Leipzig, 1927).

The Bury Abbey book came into the possession of the Knyvett family, servants to the Tudor dynasty and beneficiaries of the dissolution of the monasteries. The book was donated to the Bodleian Library, Oxford, in 1706. Its reference is MS Bodley 130 fol. 430.

The Bury book featured 142 paintings of plants (with 26 animal miniatures illustrating an appendix containing the *Bestiary of Sextus Placitus*). Some of the plant specimens are drawn from life; others are stylised representations copied from earlier manuscripts.

The plant genus *Aristolochia*, described in the example, comprises some 130 species worldwide. *Aristolochia clematitis*, a herbaceous shrub with heart-shaped leaves and yellow flowers, has become naturalised in Britain, perhaps from seeds dispersed from monastic herb gardens. *Aristolochia clematitis* (birthwort) was valued because it 'helpeth wymen to brynge furth theyr byrth'. Other species of the *Aristolochiaceae* were efficacious against a range of conditions, from snake-bite to the common cold.

The handwriting of this page of the herbal is Carolingian script of the eleventh century with rustic capital letters inherited from Rome. Carolingian attempted to revive the clear script of Roman days. Its letter-forms were copied by subsequent writing reformers and taken over by pioneer printers. Consequently this script is recognisably the same as (or not very different in its essentials from) modern typescript and the print of ordinary books (including this one). Carolingian handwriting is recommended to the beginner in palaeography as the medieval writing which presents the fewest difficulties in decipherment. The language of the herbal is the normal scientific Latin of the middle ages.

To simplify the palaeographical exercise (and our commentary) we have omitted from the explanation part of lines 1-14 and also the whole of lines 16-17. The omitted text consists of a list in two columns giving an international glossary for the plant known to the Greeks as *aristolocia* and to other nations (Italians, Dacians, Egyptians, etc) by a variety of other specific names. The writer points out that the plant 'grows in mountainous places both on unbroken and on cultivated land or on stony soil'.

Line 1 begins with capital letters **D VIM VENENI**. The first word should be **AD** and a space was left before the **D** so that at a later stage in the production process a skilled illuminator could add a suitable coloured or decorated initial. The capital **N** with its nearly horizontal crossbar superficially resembles modern capital *H*. The capitalised first words form a heading which can be translated 'against the power of venom'. Next follow two words **Herba aristolocia**. The **s** in **aristolocia** is in typical tall 'long' form (resembling *f*) and is linked to the top of **t** by ligature. The word **Herba** is dignified here and throughout the text with a large coloured uncial-form initial.

Now consider line 2. Note that medieval writers did not necessarily or clearly divide one word from another. This should present no problem when reading carefully letter by letter. Line 2 begins with a rounded letter with horizontal top stroke. This is typical medieval **t**. The second letter is made with two penstrokes: a vertical minim and a mark to its top right. This is Carolingian **r**. The top stroke of **r** runs into the simple **i** which follows. Then comes **t** again, followed by **a**. The word is **trita** meaning 'grated into powder'.

The second word consists of just one letter, a tall minim, **l** with an abbreviation stroke through its stem. Martin's *Record Interpreter* assists by showing this very common abbreviation to represent **uel** meaning 'or'. This abbreviation is a tironian note shorthand.

The third word **pisata** has a long s. It means 'ground into powder'.

The fourth word has two letters: **c** and **u**. The curved mark above **u** (the same mark as through **l** in **uel**) tells us that this is another deliberate abbreviation, here a suppressed **m**. The word is **cum**, Latin for 'with'. The Bury scribe abbreviates only sparingly, chiefly by economies in the writing of minims, especially by dropping *m*.

The fifth word begins with three minims. These could be *in, ni, ui* and so on. But read the next letters for a clue. There is a clear **e** (same form as in **Herba**), an **r** and a very clear **o**. In this context the Latin word must be **mero**, 'undiluted or pure wine'.

The sixth word is not difficult, provided the shape of round *t* is remembered and the final minims are carefully counted. The word is **potui**, 'as a draught or drink'.

The next word begins with **d** (beware of confusion between *cl* and *d* in Carolingian writing). The word is **data**, 'given'.

The last two letters on this line are **u** and **e** (the blurred top of **e** makes it resemble *c*). These two letters alone make no sense in

Latin, but taken with the first four letters on the next line which are **neno**, we read **ueneno**. Latin did not distinguish *u* and *v*: read the word therefore as **veneno**, meaning 'venom'.

The first complete word on line three begins with **r**, then **e**. Next follows long **s** (seen already in **pisata** above) with **i**. The next long **s** is linked by ligature to a letter **t**. This *st* ligature was taken up by printers and, while long *s* remained in use (that is until the nineteenth century), *st* joined together and occupied a single slug of type. Next follows an **i** (undotted as usual) and another distinctive **t**. The word is **resistit**, Latin for 'resists'.

Reading becomes easier with practice as the eye becomes familiar with the standard letter-forms and as the mind appreciates the scribe's personal quirks of penmanship or abbreviation. There are no difficult letter-forms now until perhaps line 7 and the word **aristoloci[a]e**. The tiny tag written under the final **e** indicates omission of a letter or letters. This can from the context only be an **a**, which is supplied in a square bracket to indicate something interpolated by the palaeographer on the evidence of an abbreviation mark. The termination *ae* agrees grammatically with **Herbae**, a Latin genitive or possessive case. In later medieval Latin, classical *ae* terminations were simplified to *e* without any mark of abbreviation.

In line 9 the Latin **FRIGORE**, translated by the Old English word 'ague', might refer to the chills and fevers of malaria, or perhaps to influenza or just to the common cold. It is characteristic of ancient medical practice that physicians tended to treat the symptoms observed rather than the actual cause of the illness. Thus doctors might seek to reduce the patient's temperature regardless of the cause of the fever.

In line 22 the first word is **emina[m]**. Note the abbreviation mark indicating omission of **m**. This is a medieval measure of volume (one half of a *sextarius* or about one-twelfth of a pint).

In line 27 **Aristolocia** begins with an elaborate **A** reminiscent of the display lettering of prestige texts copied in Britain and Ireland during the dark ages. It may be that this form of **A** was intended for the initial of **[A]D** in lines 1, 3, 6, 9 and 27 also. It is perhaps legitimate for the palaeographer to speculate upon why the illuminator never got around to adding the rubricated versal *A*.

The whole text reads in Latin as follows:

1. [A] D VIM VENENI. Herba aristolocia
2. trita [ue]l pisata cu[m] mero potui data. ue
3. neno resistit. [A]D FEBRES ACERRIMAS.
4. Herba aristolocia sicca suffumigabis
5. eu[m]. t[un]c hilariore[m] facies infante[m]. fugat
6. & demone[m]. [A]D FISTOLAS SANANDAS.

119

7. Herbae aristoloci[a]e radix purgata &
8. apposita. ad sanitate[m] p[er]ducit. Medici
9. uero. sine ea nichil facient. [A]D FRIGORE
10. Exustis. Herba aristolocia inoleo
11. cocta. calefactoria[m] uim habet.
12. uel cu[m] axungia porcina.
13. CONTRA SER
14. PENTIVM
15. MORSVS.
[16-17]
18. HERBAE
19. aristoloci[a]e radice[m]
20. pondus denarii
21. unius. uinum
22. emina[m] sepius bibitur. dis
23. cutit uenenum. INFANS
24. SI CONTRISTATVS
25. FVERIT. Herba aristolocia
26. suffumigabis. tunc hilariore[m] facies
27. infante[m] [A]D CANCRINOMATA. Aristolocia
28. cu[m] cypiro & draconte[a]e semen cu[m] melle im
29. positu[m]. emandat.

AGAINST THE POWER OF VENOM: the herb aristolochia, grated or ground, given as a draught in pure wine, resists venom. AGAINST THE BITTEREST FEVERS: dried aristolochia - suffumigate, and then you make the child happier. The demon flies! FOR HEALING GULLETS AND WINDPIPES: aristolochia root, cleansed and applied, brings healing. Physicians indeed can do nothing without it! AGAINST AGUE: aristolochia boiled in oil or with pork fat exerts a warming influence. AGAINST THE BITES OF SERPENTS: ... a pennyweight of aristolochia root in an emina of wine, drunk often, disperses venom. IF AN INFANT IS DISTRESSED: suffumigate with aristolochia and you make the child happier. FOR CANCERS: aristolochia with cyperus and tarragon seed in honey, when applied, effects a cure.

III CHARTER 1170
**

The estate of Marbury is situated at the centre of the rolling Cheshire plain. The place-name Marbury means 'lake-fort'. At the time of the Norman conquest in the eleventh century the fortified Saxon manor-house beside Budworth Mere commanded a landscape of mixed woodland, pasture and arable.

William the Conqueror granted extensive territories in Cheshire to his fighting companions, the Vernons of Vernon in Normandy, in return for military and administrative service rendered in the past and expected in the future. The Vernons in turn granted lesser estates and manors to their own retainers in return for similar service as and when demanded. Marbury, confiscated from its Anglo-Saxon owner, was given to Ranulph the Norman, whose son Richard of Marbury inherited in course of time.

This charter of around 1170 records the subsequent disposal of the estate by Richard of Marbury to his brother William for a one-off payment of 3.5 marks (£2.33) and a symbolic annual presentation of four barbed arrows (representing perhaps a pledge of military service) every Easter. William handed over the purchase price and was formally given possession of the manor at solemn public ceremonies firstly in the county court (in presence of the sheriff, the bishop and 'all the county of Chester'); secondly in the baronial court of his feudal lord ('my Lord Warin of Vernon'); and thirdly in the local court of the 'Wapentake of Halton'.

William and his descendants were, of course, bound to perform all requisite services to their superior lords, the Vernons, as Richard and Ranulph had previously done. Under this foundation charter the Marbury family held the estate until the late seventeenth century. An endorsement on the charter (written in a seventeenth-century hand) records that this is 'the originall dede for Merbury'.

The document is written in Latin on parchment (9½ by 5 inches; 240 by 125 mm). The foot of the document was folded over, partially obscuring the last line of the text. The fold was slit for the insertion of a parchment tag (visible at bottom centre) to which Richard of Marbury's personal seal was attached.

The charter may be dated only approximately from the style of the wording and handwriting and from the names of the persons involved. From this evidence we may date the document to around 1170.

The witnesses to the charter and to the ceremonious transfer of the property are local landowners. They do not have surnames as such at this date but are identified with the names of their manors. These men appear in other legal records of the period 1170-1212. Ralph the Chaplain was mentioned in taxation records (the pipe rolls) around 1159-62. Ralph may be the clerk who actually wrote the Marbury charter. Liulf of Twamlow is recorded as sheriff of Chester under Richard I and King John.

The handwriting is basically late twelfth-century Carolingian with some business (charter) hand developments and with angular book hand characteristics.

The first line of the charter consists of nineteen words and

A charter of 1170 recording the sale of an estate in Cheshire.

enough variety to provide the palaeographer with a working alphabet for this not-too-difficult hand. Twelve words are abbreviated by means of general or specific marks. Once this line has been mastered the whole charter can be read.

The first word consists of four letters but with a mark above to indicate an abbreviation. The first letter is difficult because it is rather unlike its modern form. The letter-form has to be remembered, perhaps by some rule such as 'if it looks like modern *H* it must be early medieval *N*'. Capitals are often problematical if only because we encounter them relatively infrequently. The second letter is **o**. This almost touches a small rounded letter at first glance resembling *c* but with a straight top-stroke. This is its confusable cousin **t**. The fourth letter is **u**. The mark above the end of the word indicates omission of **m**. The word is **Notu[m]**, 'noted'.

The second word begins with a long letter with a tiny hook to the left of its stem. This is 'long' s. The second letter is undotted **i**. (In line 2 the final word, **p[er]tinenciis**, has dots in the form of hairline acute accents over the double **i**.) The third letter, as in **Notu[m]**, is small **t** (not c). The word is **sit**, 'let it be'.

The third word is again abbreviated as the mark above indicates. The first letter is **o**. The last two letters look at first like *bz*. But *z* is almost never seen in medieval writing and the symbol here is the common standard abbreviation mark for *-us*. The middle of the

122

word consists of four minims with abbreviation mark above. These could represent *im*, *nu*, *un*, *mi*. The abbreviation cannot easily be interpreted from Martin's *Record Interpreter* because only the first letter is known. However, the palaeographer will probably know that most charters were addressed 'to all men' which, in Latin, is *omnibus*. The minims then must be **mi** and the omitted letter **n**. The word is tranliterated **om[n]ib[us]**.

The next word begins with **t** (not *c*, note the flat head). The second letter is **a**. The abbreviation mark again indicates omission of minims – here an **m**. The word is Latin **ta[m]**, 'both'.

Word five begins with a clearly evident **p**. The abbreviation mark attached to the bow of **p** is the mark numbered 3 in our chapter on abbreviations. The symbol indicates omission of **re**. The next letter was in **sit**. It is long s. Then comes **e**, two minims for **n**, and small flat-topped **t** (by now the reader will have stopped confusing it with *c*). The **i** which follows is undotted.

Then comes an apparent *bz* which we now know to be **b[us]**. The whole word reads **p[re]sentib[us]**, 'present'.

Now comes yet another abbreviated word, written with just one letter, **q**. This is modified with a mark through the tail as well as a superscript **a** with dashing headstroke. Martin's *Record Interpreter* gives us **q[uam]**, 'and', which normally means 'than' but combined with *tam* denotes 'as well as' or simply 'and'.

The seventh word begins with **f**. At first glance this seems to resemble long *s*, but differs in its cross-stroke to the right of the stem. The next letter is **u** followed by the confusable **t**, an undotted minim for **i** and long **s** (not *f*). The abbreviation sign (which we numbered 4 in our chapter) indicates omission of **ur**. The word is **fut[ur]is**, 'future'.

The eighth word is an abbreviation beginning with unamended **q** and followed by amended **d**. Martin tells us that this must be **q[uo]d**, 'that'.

The next word begins with **e**. The middle letter is **g** with its very characteristic tail. The third letter is **o**. The word, **ego**, means 'I'.

Words ten to twelve are the names of the donor. **RicaRd'** is clearly written with lettering for emphasising the dignity of a lord of the manor. The final mark indicates that the Latin masculine termination **-us** has been dropped. Next comes **de**, 'of'. The surname begins with a form of capital **M** (distinguished from small *m* by a definite trailing third leg). The next letter is **e**, followed by an ordinary small **r**, then another **e**. The **b** and **i** are clear. The next letter with a tail below the line may cause a little difficulty. It is **r** written in a manner that recalls Anglo-Saxon spiky minuscule *r*. This long *r* flourished throughout the middle ages in companion-ship with forms of small *r*. The final letter **a** gives **Merebira**, 'Marbury'. This earliest form of the place-name is important for historians because it reflects the original meaning of *mere*, 'lake', more clearly than the modern form of the name.

The thirteenth word is clearly written and unabbreviated with tall **d**, normal **e**, tall **d** again and undotted **i** to give **dedi**, meaning 'have given'.

The next word is a common tironian note abbreviation for **et** which might be translated in full as 'and' or, to preserve a sense of the original, as our own abbreviation sign **&**.

The fifteenth word begins with a sign resembling a number *9*. This is the standard abbreviation (number 6 in the chapter on abbreviation) for **con**. Then follows a rounded small **c** (contrast with flat-topped *t* in **Notu[m]**). Then comes **e** and two long letters (as in the fifth and seventh words) namely a double long **s**, followed by **i**. The word is **[con]cessi**, 'have granted'.

The next word begins with a large and elegant letter which we guess to be a capital letter, presumably for a proper name. This is an especially difficult initial letter-form, which just has to be learned and remembered. It appears on page 52 of Johnson and Jenkinson's *English Court Hand*. The letter is **W**. Next follows **ll**. The line through the tall ascending strokes indicates an abbreviation. The last letter written is small **o**. The name written is **Wllo**. This is one of the most common (and best-known) Norman names

– obviously 'William' in its Latin form **W[i]ll[elm]us** here ending in the dative **o** to mean 'to William'. Other Latin forms of William met with in medieval writings are *Guillelmus* and *Gulielmus*.

The seventeenth word begins with **f** (not long *s*), followed by small **r** and a minim for **i**. The mark above is the all-purpose mark of abbreviation. Martin's *Record Interpreter* suggests **fratri** (dative, 'to the brother') as a possibility. By now, the beginner will have a feeling for the use of abbreviation signs and not expect always that the all-purpose mark represents missing minims. *Fratri* could be arrived at without Martin's help by considering suitable common Latin words beginning with *fr* and capable of ending in *i*. The sense of the line, too, would confirm 'brother' as correct.

The penultimate word, clearly written, is **meo**, 'my'.

The final word in the line is the same as the eleventh word, **de**, 'of'.

1. Notu[m] sit om[n]ib[us] ta[m] p[re]sentib[us] q[uam] fut[ur]is q[uo]d ego RicaRd[us] de Merebira dedi [et] [con]cessi W[i]ll[elm]o fr[atr]i meo de

2. merebiria [et] hac mea p[re]senti carta [con]firmaui tota[m] terra[m] de Merebir[a] cu[m] om[n]ib[us] p[er]tinenciis

3. suis in bosco in plano in p[ra]tis in pascuis in Molendinis in viuariis [et] in om[n]ib[us] aliis locis

4. ad eande[m] uilla[m] p[er]tinentib[us] libera[m] [et] q[ui]eta[m] [et] soluta[m] a me [et] heredib[us] meis sibi [et] heredibus

5. suis tenenda[m] [et] hab[e]nda[m] in feodu[m] [et] hereditate[m] inp[er]petuu[m]. redd[e]ndo m[ihi] [et] heredib[us] meis

6. ip[s]e et heredes sui annuati[m] ad pasca q[ua]tuor sagittas barbatas p[ro] om[n]i seruicio m[ihi] [et] here-

7. dib[us] meis p[er]tinente. Ita q[ui]de[m] q[uod] p[re]dictus W[i]ll[elmu]s fr[ater] meus idde[m] seruicium facere debet d[omi]no

8. GWaR[ino] d[e] uornon' q[uo]d egomet feci d[omi]no meo u[e]l pater meus ante me fecit d[omi]nis suis. Hoc

9. aute[m] feci [con]s[e]nsu [et] [con]cessu d[omi]ni GWaR[ini] de uornon [et]   heredor[um] meor[um]. & depono a me [et] here-

10. dib[us] meis om[n]e ius meu[m] de tera pr[re]dicta Will[elm]o fr[atr]i meo p[re]dicto [et] heredib[us] suis in p[er]petuu[m]

11. p[ro] trib[us] marcis [et] dimid[ia]. q[ua]s Will[elmu]s fr[ate]r meus p[re]dict[us] dedit m[ihi]. parte[m] cora[m] om[n]i comitatu cestrie

12. [et] parte[m] in curia d[omi]ni mei GWaR[ini] de vornon [et] parte[m] cora[m] Wapentach de hatheltona. Teste

13. Lidulfo de tWamlaWe. Hamone de Borthintona. Gileb[erto] fil[io] Nigell[i]. Rob[erto] de Stochal'. Rad[ulpho] capell[ano].
14. Ric[ardo] de vornon. Raer de stanthurn. Gileb[er]to de bostoc. [et] om[n]i comitatu cestrie.

Let it be noted by all men both present and future that I Richard of Marbury have given and granted to William my brother of Marbury – and by this my present charter have confirmed – the whole land of Marbury with all its appurtenances in woodland, in open ground, in meadows, in pastures, in mills, in fish-ponds and in all other places belonging to the same township. To hold and to have to him and his heirs, in fee and by inheritance for ever, freely and quietly and undisturbed by me and my heirs; he and his heirs rendering to me and my heirs, yearly at Easter, four barbed arrows for all service appertaining to me and my heirs. But on condition that the aforesaid William my brother should perform the same service to the Lord Warin of Vernon that I myself did to my lord or my father before me did to his lords. This I did by consent and grant of the Lord Warin of Vernon and of my heirs. And I transfer from me and my heirs all my right in the land aforesaid to William my brother aforesaid and his heirs for ever for three and a half marks which William my brother aforesaid gave to me, part in the presence of all the county of Chester and part in the court of the Lord Warin of Vernon and part in the presence of the Wapentake of Halton. With these witnesses: Liulf of Twemlow, Hamo of Bartington, Gilbert son of Nigell, Robert of Stochal, Ralph the chaplain, Richard of Vernon, Raer of Stanthorne, Gilbert of Bostock and all the county of Chester.

IV CHARTER 1268
****

The burgh of Elgin in Moray was founded as an administrative and commercial centre of Norman power during the twelfth century. The town was planned in the usual medieval pattern around a broad high street or market-place with a royal castle just beyond the burgh boundary. Elgin and some thirty other royal burghs were established by the Norman kings of Scots, David I and William I, to control and feudalise the Celtic clansmen of the burghal hinterland. Elgin was populated at first with immigrant merchant families from Normandy, Flanders, England and Picardy. The townsfolk (burgesses) were endowed with extensive lands, trading monopolies and tax advantages. The burgesses were permitted to combine in a merchant guild for the better governance of the community and the regulation of its trade.

In 1268, while King Alexander III and his court were ensconced in the royal castle at Elgin, the burgh provost, bailies, councillors and burgesses obtained a charter recognising the existence of their guild merchant. The charter was a public document, open for all to see and addressed 'to all upright men of our whole land'.

The charter was written in ink on parchment. The writer was probably one of the clerks of the royal Chancery who accompanied the king as he toured his realm. The scribe wrote in his normal business hand of the royal court of Scotland. The parchment was folded over and slit at the bottom to allow a parchment tag to be threaded through the foot of the document. The king's seal was fixed to this tag.

This charter remained in the town's muniment chest (known as the *burgh cadget*) for seven hundred years. When the administrative functions of royal burghs were abolished in 1975 the charter passed to the new Moray District Council, in whose record office at the Tolbooth, Forres, the document is now securely stored under the reference ZBE1 A1/1.

At first glance, perhaps, the handwriting seems difficult. Certainly the numerous floreations of thirteenth-century writing complicate the task of decipherment. However, once the reader is able to separate the various tags, notches and abbreviation marks from the basic letter-forms the script is not difficult to read.

During the thirteenth century, written documents became more and more usual as evidence of title to property or entitlement to privilege. The writers who acted on behalf of kings and landowners were generally men in holy orders, that is priests and monks. These churchmen (clerics, clerks for short) could usually write fluent Latin. Clerks were taught to write swiftly and to abbreviate wherever possible. Thus in line 1 of the Elgin charter nine out of fourteen words were shortened in some way.

The first word is **Alex**, the name of the king. The only difficult letter in the word is the **x** which drops a descender below the line. The hooked horizontal line above the word indicates an abbreviation. The full name is Alexander. This (Greek) Christian name was introduced into Scotland under the influence of the saintly Queen Margaret (1047-93), wife of Malcolm Canmore, King of Scots. She was an Anglo-Saxon princess who grew up in the Hungarian court. Her son was christened Alexander in deference to Pope Alexander II.

The second word is also abbreviated (note the floreated mark above). The first letter is difficult and must be looked up in a suitable palaeographical textbook such as Johnson and Jenkinson, *English Court Hand*, where (on page 13) this letter is reproduced. It is a dignified initial (capital) letter **D**. These initials, which we would transcribe as capital letters, can often be problematical on

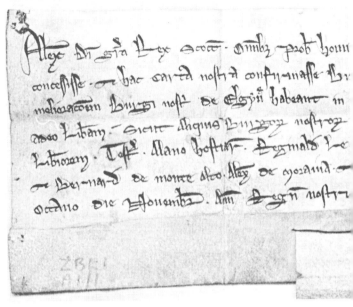

account of their many extra flourishes. The second letter is a small **i** with no very evident dot above. Martin's *Record Interpreter* extends this abbreviation for us into **Dei**, the Latin for 'of God'.

The third word commences with another difficult letter with a strange beaver tail below. This could be an elaborate *S*, but in this case is **g**. (Beaver-tailed *s* and *g* are famously confusable.) The next letter is a short open **r**. The final letter is simple **a** (known as single-storeyed *a* because it lacks an ascending stroke or second bow on top). The fancy 'papal-knot' abbreviation mark above the word indicates an unspecified omission of letters between **r** and **a**. Martin's *Record Interpreter* again comes to the rescue with *gratia* meaning 'by the grace'. We have preferred the alternative, perhaps more common, medieval spelling with **c** as **gracia.**

The fourth word is written in full. It begins with capital **R** (just barely decipherable through its problematical flourishes and distortions). The next two letters were seen before in the king's name. They are **ex**, completing **Rex**, Latin for 'king'.

The fifth word begins with the confusable *g* or *s*. We can guess that in this case it is **s** because we expect some reference to Scotland. The rest of the word looks just like two pairs of spectacles. These shapes are made by closely written **c** plus **o** and **t** plus **t**. This shows how nearly indistinguishable are medieval *c* and

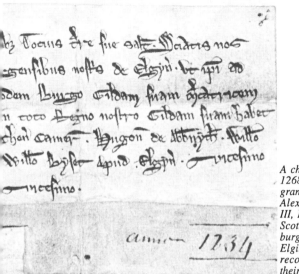

A charter of 1268 granted by Alexander III, King of Scots, to his burgesses of Elgin, recognising their guild merchant.

rounded *t*. The word as written is **scott**, again with abbreviation mark to indicate that something is missed off the end, here a Latin termination in the genitive case to give **scottorum**, 'of the Scots'.

The sixth word begins with a capital **O** distinguished by a couple of vertical lines. Next come four minims and an abbreviation mark. The letters are **m** with **i**. The abbreviation mark indicates omission of a couple of minims making **n**. Next comes **b** with a notched and floreated ascender. The final letter is a special sign used to indicate the common Latin ending *-us*. The whole word, with omissions supplied in square brackets, is **Om[n]ib[us]** meaning 'to all' or 'for all'.

The next word begins with a moderately floreated **p**, followed by a small round **r** (shaped something like a figure 2). Next come **o** and **b**, both reasonably easy to decipher despite the confusion which is introduced by floreation of the *b* ascender and the straight line abbreviation mark at the end of the word. The word, extended, is **prob[is]**, 'upright', as in the English 'probity'.

In the eighth word the initial **h** should give few problems (despite floreations). As with many of the convoluted initial letters, the palaeographer must decide whether to transliterate lower-case **h** or whether the degree of floreation (coupled with the form of letter) justifies use of upper-case *H*. The **o** which follows is straightforward. Less simple to decipher are the seven minims which come

129

next. The scribe, appreciating our difficulty, has helped out by adding very clear slanting hairline marks above the fourth minim. This is the medieval form of the dot above *i*. The three preceding minims must be **m**. The last three minims are **ni** (note the hairline accent for **i** which has strayed to the far side of the ascender of the next letter, which is **b**). The final sign (like a figure 3 with a straggling tail) stands for *-us*. The word is **hominib[us]** 'men'. We might have guessed this from *probis*, knowing that the common form for charters was an address to 'to all upright men'.

The floreated first letter of the ninth word, elaborated with a vertical stroke, is **T**. The **o** which follows is straightforward. The **ci** which come next are in the usual linked form with a hairline stroke to dot the **i**. Two minims follow, linked at the base into **u**. The final letter **s** is written in closed-up form (something like a figure 8). The word is **Tocius**, 'whole'.

The tenth word begins with a rounded letter with horizontal head-stroke, an obvious **t**. The second letter was in *gracia* – an **r**. Next an **e** as in *Alex*. The knotted sign (also in *gracia*) above the word indicates an omission between **t** and **r**, here of the letters **er**. The Latin word is **t[er]re**, meaning 'of the land'. Classical Latin (the kind learned in school) would use the form *terrae* but medieval Latinists dispensed with the *a*.

The long floreated letter beginning the eleventh word is another standard form of the initial letter of *scottorum* – an **s**. This long *s* is common in old handwriting and is easily confused with *f*. The chief real difference between the two is in the tiny cross-stroke which in long *s* extends only to the left of the stem but in *f* crosses the stem. The word, in full, is **sue** 'of his'.

The twelfth word also begins with *s* in the *scottorum* form. Other letters in the word are clear, though with two abbreviations. Martin's *Record Interpreter* may again be called for. On the other hand the word is part of the common-form wording of royal charters and might be guessed as **sal[u]t[em]**, 'greeting'.

The thirteenth word begins with *s* in a form which demands transliteration in capital form, and, as usual with capital forms, the letter is not easy to unravel from its floreations. It is the only **S** of this form in the document and the charter offers no internal comparators. Johnson and Jenkinson's book is again called for. Next is **ci**, again written close together (to look like a flat-headed *a*). Then follows **a** in a typical form with a main stroke rising high above the closed bow. Next comes another closed figure, perhaps *ci* again or, in this case, **ti**. Finally comes **s** in the *salutem* form. The word is **Sciatis**, written in full, meaning 'know ye'.

The fourteenth word begins with **n** plus **o** and finishes with the *salutem* form of **s**. The final letter is slightly dignified (because it is at the end of the line) with an elongated top stroke. The Latin word **nos** means 'we'.

The first line should give the reader a sufficient start and experience of the main thirteenth-century letter-forms to proceed to transliterate the rest of the charter. This first line gives examples of seventeen small letters of the alphabet (some such as **a** and **s** in more than one form) and also half a dozen capital letters. The only important letters not in line 1 are *f* and *d* and these appear in line 2, *f* in the sixth word *confirmasse* and *d* in the ninth word *de*. It should be possible now to complete the document but a few further hints may prove helpful.

In lines 5-6 are set out the names of witnesses to the charter. They are all men and all courtiers who accompanied the king on his travels. Their names begin with convoluted capitals. Their Christian names are of Breton or Norman origin (though we might now think of them as typically Scottish, such was the extent of the Normanisation of the kingdom). Their surnames derive from place-name and job titles. The king's companions include Alan the doorward, steward or *hostiarius* of Scotland, sometime regent of the kingdom. He was the king's brother-in-law, lord of the estate of Lundie. Alan's descendants still bear the surname Durward. Another witness is Hugh, lord of Abernethy on Tay. William and Bernard *de monte alto* were descendants of Hugo, a Norman immigrant who enjoyed the lordship 'of the high hill'. In Hugo's time the place was known by its Norman-French title as *le mont hault*. The place-name is now corrupted to Mold and the surname to Mowatt.

In lines 6 and 7 there is a calligraphic flourish before the Latin word *vicesimo*, 'the twentieth'. This sign does not seem to require transliteration, because it is only a flourish – not a letter, word or mark of abbreviation. This flourish can be distinguished from the somewhat similar symbol used in lines 2 and 6 for the Latin *et*, 'and', which should be transliterated as **et**, **[et]** or **&**.

The date 1234 written at the foot of the charter has clearly been added at a later time, from the appearance of the handwriting, the cut of the pen and the colour of the ink. It was added by a well-meaning antiquarian. Unfortunately (but not uninterestingly) the date 1234 is incorrect! We know this because one of the witnesses named in the charter, Reginald Le Chen, the king's chamberlain, held this top financial office only for a brief period from 1267 until 1269. The charter was written in the twentieth year of King Alexander; but which Alexander? Both Alexander II and Alexander III ruled for more than twenty years. It was Alexander III who ruled in the period 1267-9. The twentieth year of his reign was 1268 (when Reginald was the royal chamberlain). The charter can therefore be dated to 1268. In analysing problems such as this the palaeographer enters the challenging realm of the diplomatist.

1. Alex[ander] D[e]i gr[aci]a Rex scott[orum]. Om[n]ib[us] prob[is] hominib[us] Tocius t[er]re sue sal[u]t[em]. Sciatis nos

2. concessisse. et hac Carta nostra confirmasse Burgensibus nost[ri]s de Elgyn'. vt ip[s]i ad

3. meliorac[i]o[n]em Burgi nost[ri] de Elgyn' habeant in eodem Burgo Gildam suam M[er]catricem

4. adeo Lib[er]am. – sicut Aliquis Burgo[rum] nostro[rum] in toto Regno nostro Gildam suam habet

5. Lib[er]iorem. Test[ibus]. Alano hostiar[io]. Reginald[o] Le Chen' Camer[ario]. Hugon[e] de Abb[ir]nyth'. Will[elm]o

6. et Bernard[o] de monte Alto. Alex[andro] de Morauia. et Will[elm]o Byset Apud Elgyn'. vicesimo

7. Octauo die Nouembr[is]. Ann[o] Regn[i] nostri. vicesimo.

8. Anno 1234

Alexander, by the grace of God King of Scots, to all upright men of his whole land, greeting. Know that we have granted and by this our charter have confirmed to our burgesses of Elgin that, for the improvement of our burgh of Elgin, they should have in the same burgh their guild merchant – as freely as any of our burgesses in our whole kingdom has his guild. With witnesses: Alan the Doorward; Reginald Le Chen, chamberlain; Hugh of Abernethy; William and Bernard of Mold; Alexander of Moray; and William Byset. At Elgin, on the twenty-eighth day of November in the twentieth year of our reign.

In the year 1234

V LETTER PATENT 1393
****

This document of 1393 is of a type known as a **letter patent** because it was issued patent, that is open, for all to see. Though an item of correspondence, the letter was not enclosed in an envelope but was on the contrary a very public sort of communication specifically addressed 'to all men'.

During the late fourteenth century the Dunbars, as Earls of Moray, had replaced the kings of Scots as feudal lords of the (former royal) burgh of Elgin. Through their burgesses, they enjoyed the financial advantages of a monopoly of trade within a broad economic zone (almost half of the old county of Elginshire) with the burgh at its centre. The Dunbars and the Elgin burgesses also enjoyed certain exemptions in respect of goods exported through the burgh's port at the mouth of the river Spey. In 1392 a new earl, Thomas, succeeded to the title. He took an active interest in his burgh of Elgin, noting the dilapidations caused by recurrent plague, civil disorder, ineffectual central government and economic recession. In 1393 he issued this letter patent in favour of his burgesses, dealing with the important matter of their export trade.

The document was written by a clerk in the Dunbar household, or perhaps even by the town clerk of Elgin, in a typical business hand of the period. The scribe wrote swiftly and joined some of the letters together. He attempted to dignify some of his letter-forms by adopting book-hand characteristics, though in general he strayed little from the normal administrative hand of his day.

The document was written on parchment which was cut at the foot to form a tag to which the modest seal of Thomas Dunbar was attached. The seal is now missing, though a slight staining of the tag shows where it was attached.

The text was written in the form of English known as Middle English. This was the language of the Scottish burghs and of the Scottish royal court at Edinburgh, though in rural districts, especially in the highlands and islands, Gaelic predominated. Middle English in its various dialects was, of course, the language of much of England too. Students who have read Chaucer's *Canterbury Tales* and Langland's *Piers Plowman* will feel quite at home with the grammar, vocabulary and diction of this contemporary Scottish charter. Middle English words, pronunciation and modes of expression supplied many of the elements which have made Scottish dialect so distinctive.

Line 1 begins with **C**, which is a paragraph mark representing the Latin *capitulum*, 'chapter' or 'paragraph'. The reader's eye becomes accustomed to the handwriting after the first couple of words, which clearly read **Be it**. In the third word **Knawyn**, 'known', there are two letters which cause difficulties even for experienced palaeographers. The letters *K* and *k* are notoriously problematical in old handwritings – and doubly so here because in a dignified initial form which transcribes as **K**. Small **w** is in typical form with two curved ascenders. The sixth word **men** ends in a calligraphic flourish which throws a tail beneath the word. (A similar flourish completes *men* at the end of line 5.) The eighth word begins with the same letter as appears penultimately in *Knawyn* – **y**. Here, though, it stands for the Old English runic letter *thorn* representing *th*. The eighth word is therefore **this**: the **y** has a dot above and **i** is accented with a curved hairline stroke. Elsewhere in the charter the scribe uses *th*, as in **vthir**, 'other', (line 3) rather than *y* or thorn. The ninth word is abbreviated with a particular sign showing omission of **re** from **p[re]sent**; the word ends in a downward flourish. The eleventh word **Vs**, 'us', is the

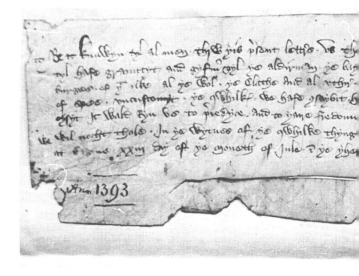

royal 'we', which Thomas Dunbar, as a mere earl, might not be deemed strictly entitled to use! The use of 'us' (where modern grammar requires 'we') was acceptable correct usage in Middle English – and survives in some modern English dialects.

In line 2 the eighth word **aldirman** is an English term (from Old English *Ealdorman*, 'tribal or communal elder'). The word refers to a senior town councillor and was used in Scotland for the headman of a burgh in documents written in English. In Latin documents the word *prepositus* was employed – a word which gave rise to the English (and Scots) word 'provost'. This was the usual title for the burgh headman (equivalent to the English mayor) until burghs were abolished in 1975. The tenth word **baylis** refers to the bailies or senior magistrates who held court as sheriffs within the liberties of the burgh.

In line 3 the first word, **burges**, refers to the 'burgesses or merchant freemen', the hundred or so leading merchants who controlled the town's trade. The first letter of the third word is again **y** followed by a small superscript **t**. The y[t] abbreviation for 'that' is very common but each palaeographer must decide how it should be transliterated. The fourth word, **ilke**, is everyday Middle English. For interpretation the reader turns to Stratmann's *Middle-English Dictionary* or even to the ordinary *Oxford English Dictionary*. *Ilk*, meaning 'same' is still used today by poets seeking the

134

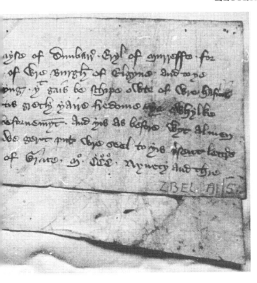

A letter patent on parchment by Thomas Dunbar, Earl of Moray, dated 1393, granting freedom from customs duties to the burgesses of Elgin.

special effect of an archaic word and by Scotsmen in everyday speech. The final word in line 3 is **hafine**, 'haven, harbour'. This was written over an erasure; one of the erased letters was an **i** whose looped accent is evident.

In line 4 the reader should find few difficulties until the eighth word, which begins with a standard medieval mark of abbreviation for *con-*, usually in Latin words, but equally useful for an English word. The word **[con]saybit**, 'conceived', is spelled as pronounced at the time, the fourteenth century. The final word is legible enough as **qwhylke**, though a suitable dictionary (or familiarity with spoken Scots) will be required to find its modern equivalent, 'which'!

In line 5 the first word is **oysyt**, 'used'. The fourth word begins with **R** (distorted to something like a **P** shape). The word is **Ryn**, 'run, bring'. The next word, **vs**, for 'us', has a typical form of *v* with looped ascender. The rules for using *u* or *v* were not clearly defined (in Latin there is only one letter and so the problem does not arise). In English writings *u* and *v* might be used as vowel or consonant. Dunbar's clerk seems to prefer *v* to begin a word – except where for special emphasis he throws in a *w*, as in line 6, **wre seel**, 'our seal'! The *v* provides the basic letter which is 'doubled' by addition of an extra ascender (look back to *Knawyn* in line 1 and *wre* in line 2).

135

In line 6 the fourth word, **thole**, is a usual Middle English for 'tolerate'. The **h** drops its right leg below the line in a manner which was a feature (in increasingly straggling fashion) of small *h* until the seventeenth century. The thirteenth word, **gerit**, (with figure-8 small *g*, backward-rolling high bowed *e*, open-splayed *r*, minimalist *i*) is from the Middle English verb *gar*, 'to cause'.

The year in line 7 appears as **M°**, an abbreviation for Latin **Millesimo** 'one thousandth', followed by **C°** for **Centesimo**, 'one hundredth' (repeated three times for 'three hundredth'). The writer is thinking in Latin ordinal numbers so the year is the 'one thousand three hundredth' year of grace. He then drops into simple English and abandons that grammatical construction in favour of a simple cardinal number, **nynety and thre** (ninety-three).

The pencilled record office reference appears at bottom right (ZBE1 A1/3). Record office references relate to the nature and provenance of a document. This typical reference may be interpreted from the office classification scheme thus: Z, local authority collections; B, burgh muniments; E1, Elgin; A, town clerk's department; 1, charters; /3, third in the series.

At bottom left an antiquarian of the eighteenth century has added, in his own ink and handwriting, the date 1393. These subsequent additions are all interesting to the palaeographer because they provide clues to the history of the document in the centuries after it was written in terms of its custody (and thus perhaps also its authenticity) and the interest it has attracted in the past.

Middle English

1. C Be it Knawyn tyl al men. thrw yis p[re]sent lettr'e. Vs thomayse of Dunbarr'. Eryl of Murreffe. for
2. tyl hafe grauntyt and gyfin' Tyl ye aldirman. ye baylis. of wre Burgh' of Elgyne. and to ye
3. burges. of y[a]t ilke al ye wol. ye Clathe and al vthir' thyng[is]. yat gais be schipe owte of wre hafine
4. of spee. vncustomyt. ye qwhilk'. we hafe [con]saybit. hurtis gretly yaire fredome ye qwhylke
5. oysyt It wald Ryn vs to p[re]iedyce. and to yaire fredome befornemyt'. and yis as before wyt al men
6. we wil nocht thole. In ye wytnes of ye qwhilke thyng[is]. we gerit put wre seel to yis p[re]sent lettr's
7. at Elgyne xxiij day of ye Moneth of Iule. i[n] ye yhere of Grace. M°C°C°C°. Nynety and thre

Modern English

Be it known to all men through this present letter: We Thomas of Dunbar, Earl of Moray, have granted and given to the alderman, the bailies of our Burgh of Elgin and to all the burgesses of that same place – all the wool, the cloth and all other things that go by ship out of our haven of Spey free of customs duties. The which we have conceived greatly hurts their freedom; the which, if done, would be as prejudicial to us as to their freedom aforesaid. And this as before with all men we will not tolerate. In witness of which things we have caused our seal to be put to this present letter, at Elgin, on the twenty-third day of the month of July in the year of grace one thousand three hundred and ninety-three.

VI THEOLOGICAL COMMENTARY 1400
*****

In informal academic book hand; on parchment; from the binding of Elgin burgh court book, Moray District Record Office, Forres, ZBE1 B2/3.

This fragment is from a commentary on the *Summa Theologiae* of Thomas Aquinas, 'the prince of scholastic theologians'.

Aquinas was born in Italy in 1226. As a student in Paris he was introduced to Aristotle's philosophy by the Dominican academic Albertus Magnus. Aquinas's subsequent academic career included lectureships at Cologne, Rome and Naples. His *Summa*, which remained uncompleted at his death in 1274, was a stupendous attempt to systematise Christian theology in scholastic question-and-answer form. Aquinas was canonised St Thomas in 1323.

Generations of scholars produced thousands of commentaries on the *Summa*. The names of some commentators (Henry of Ghent, Giles of Rome, Peter of Tarentaise) are well-known. Other commentaries, anonymous and incomplete, are referred to by cataloguers simply as *fragmenta quaestionum theologicarum*.

The fragment reproduced is from a commentary on the first half of the second part (prima secundae, 1a2ae) of *Summa* which deals with 'God as the End of Man'. The commentator tackles *Quaestio*11 *De Fruitione*, 'On Enjoyment', especially Articles 3 and 4 which ask whether enjoyment 'is only of an ultimate end .... and only of an end possessed'.

This commentary, composed perhaps as early as the 1320s, may derive from a famous lecture, probably delivered at an Albertine school such as Louvain or Cologne. The professor's discourse was copied in book form for wider dissemination. Even these few lines from a long and complex discourse demonstrate the medieval delight in subtle rhetorical disputations on essential questions. The author, a profound thinker of no little poetic imagination, builds his argument around the metaphor of tree and fruit, while playing a game of significant word-association with *fruicio*, 'enjoyment/ fruition', and *fructus*, 'fruit'.

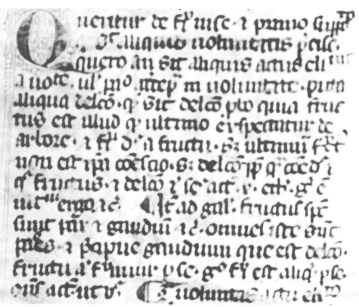

A fragment from a commentary on the 'Summa Theologiae' of Thomas Aquinas, about 1400.

The discourse was clearly intended for advanced students – bachelors of philosophy and theologians already well versed in the works of Aristotle and Aquinas, and so attuned to their teacher's thesis and style that the drastic economies of the scribe's abbreviative excess would present no difficulty or ambiguity. The modern reader who lacks a background in medieval theology may find difficulty in getting started on this kind of palaeographical exercise.

This edition was made around 1400. It is written in the informal book hand of an academic copyist after the manner of a scholastic (rather than bureaucratic) writing-room. The international literary script blends French, Netherlandish and English influences. The book was clearly a prestige production, the product of much labour and care. The text is written in double columns on good quality white parchment and enlivened with painted illuminations, decorated initials and alternating red and blue *capitulum* marks.

It is not known what happened to this book from 1400 until around 1585 when this single leaf was used to make a cover for the court book of the burgh of Elgin in Moray. It is very possible that the book had come to Scotland intact as the gift of a pious benefactor or scholarly canon to the library of Elgin cathedral. On the other hand, the text may have travelled to Elgin in fragments after the Reformation – scraps of popish anachronism, the stock-in-trade of an enterprising waste-parchment merchant.

1. Queritur de f[r]vi[cione] inse. [et] primo suppo[si]to
2. q[uod] s[i]t aliquid uoluntatis p[re]cise.
3. quero an sit aliquis actus eli[ci]tus
4. a uo[lunta]te. u[e]l pa[ssi]o ar[e]cep[ta] in uoluntate. puta
5. aliqua del[ecta]c[i]o. q[uod] sit del[ecta]c[i]o p[ro]bo quia fruc
6. tus est illud q[uod] ultimo exspectatur de
7. arbore. [et] f[r]vi[cio] d[atur] a fructu. S[ed] ultimu[m] f[r]uct[us]
8. non est ip[s]a co[m]escio. S[ed] del[ecta]c[i]o p[ro]p[ter] q[uam] co[m]ed[itur] [et]
9. q[ueritur] fructus. [et] del[ecta]c[i]o [eciam] se[quitur] act[um] .x. eth[ice]. [i]g[itur] est
10. ult[imum] ergo [et]c[etera]. C[apitulum] It[em] ad gal[atas]. fructus sp[iri]t[us]
11. sunt pax [et] gaudiu[m] [et]c[etera]. omnes iste su[n]t
12. pa[ssi]o[n]es. [et] p[re]cipue gaudium que est del[ecta]c[i]o.
13. fructu a[utem] f[r]vimur p[er]se. [er]go f[r]vi[cio] est aliq[uid] p[er]se.-
14. [con][seque]ns act[um]. ut v[idetur].   ....

On the question of the nature of enjoyment, and, by first hypothesis, that it may be something of the will precisely: I ask whether it may be any act elicited by the will, or some passive quality received in the will.

Put the case of any kind of delight: I judge that it may be a delight because fruit is that which is ultimately expected from a tree – and enjoyment is given by fruit. However, the ultimate end of fruit is not the meal itself, but the delight on account of which the fruit is consumed and sought. And so delight follows on an act. 10th book of *Ethics* 'hence this is therefore an ultimate end ...' and so on. Moreover, according to *Galatians* 'the fruits of the Spirit are peace and joy ...' and so on. All of these are passive states of being – and especially joy, which is a delight. However, from fruit we derive an intrinsic enjoyment. Therefore enjoyment is something of itself – consequent upon an act – as it seems.

In line 1 the initial letter of **Queritur** is coloured blue, its pen-drawn decoration in red extending down the margin of the paragraph. In **f[r]vi[cione]** the scribe employs a characteristic abbreviated form for *fruicio*, 'enjoyment', while, to avoid confusion, *fructus*, 'fruit', is written in full (lines 5-6, 7, 9, 10, 13). **V** and **u** are used interchangeably, the scribe preferring a **v** for an abbreviative superscript vowel in *frvicione* and **u** for an initial consonant in *uoluntatis*.

In line 4 the mark below the initial letter of **ar[e]cep[ta]** is a *punctum delens* inserted to expunge the letter **a**, leaving **recepta**.

In line 9 **.x. eth[ice]** refers to book 10 of Aristotle's *Nicomachean Ethics*, which concerns 'Pleasure' (for an English translation see the World's Classics edition by D. Ross, London, 1954).

Halfway through line 10 the **C[apitulum]** mark indicates the opening of a new paragraph; **ad gal[atas]** refers to St Paul's epistle to the Galatians 5:22-23: 'But the fruit of the Spirit is love, joy, peace, longsuffering ...'. Highlighted in blue ink, **fructus** may be singular or plural.

VII MANOR COURT ROLL 1438
****

In mongrel hand; on parchment; Norfolk Record Office, MS 6020, 16B5

The lord of the manor enjoyed a proprietorial interest in the people and property of his (or her) estates. The manor court of Antingham in Norfolk, held for the lady Joan Wichingham of Witchingham Magna on 17th September 1438, acted on information received against Richard Jonyour. He was accused of neglecting his house – a structure of timber-framing, with wattle-and-daub infilling and a thatched roof. A marginal note (not transcribed) shows John amerced (fined) in the substantial sum of 6d.

An extract from the manor court roll of Antingham, Norfolk, 17th September 1438.

1. C[apitulum] Cur[ia] ib[ide]m tent[a] die m[er]cur[ii]
   p[ro]x[ima] post f[estu]m Exaltac[i]o[n]is s[an]c[t]e Cruc[is]
   a[nn]o r[egni] r[egis] henr[ici] sexti xvijmo
2. C[apitulum] Iur[atores] ex offic[i]o p[re]s[entant] q[uo]d
   Ric[ard]us Ionyo[ur] g[r]auit[er] vastauit mes[suagium]
   suu[m] de villen[agio] d[omi]ni in antyngham ita q[uo]d
   su[n]t in p[er]iculo
3. cadere p[ro] defectu tectur[e] daubur[e] [et] carpentar[ie]
   I[de]o in m[isericord]ia. Et p[receptum] est ei d[i]c[tu]m
   mes[suagium] bene [et] sufficient[er] rep[er]ar[e] cit[r]a
   p[ro]x[imam] Cur[iam] sub pe[n]a
4. vj s' viij d' Et Quia impotens est d[i]c[tu]m ten[ementum]
   rep[er]ar[e] ut dicit[ur] I[de]o p[receptum] est s[ei]s[i]re in
   man[um] d[omi]ne [et]c[etera]

Paragraph: Court held there [Antingham] on Wednesday next
after the feast of the elevation of the holy cross in the seventeenth
year of the reign of King Henry the sixth

Paragraph: Jurors by virtue of office present that Richard Jonyour
has gravely wasted his messuage of the villeinage of the lord [of
the manor] in Antingham which thus are in danger of falling down
for want of roofing, plastering and carpentry: And it is commanded
to him well and sufficiently to repair the said messuage before the
next court under penalty of 6s 8d. And because he is unable to
repair the said tenement, as it is said, therefore it is commanded to
take possession into the hand of the lady [of the manor] etc. ...

Line 1: the paragraph mark (also line 2) is derived from a
stylised **C** for *Capitulum* 'chapter'; the line is finished with a
scribal flourish.

Line 2: the 'lord' (**d[omi]ni**) of Antingham was at this time a
lady (**d[omi]ne** line 4).

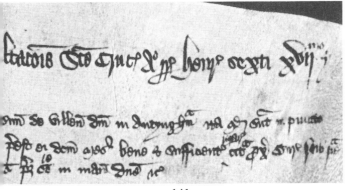

Line 3: **rep[er]ar[e]** is inserted with caret below; the reading of this cramped insertion is assisted by **rep[er]ar[e]** (line 4); the tironian note for **et** is typical but noteworthy.

Line 4: **Et** is inserted without caret; **in man[um]** unspecific mark of abbreviation allows equally *man[us], man[u]* or *man[ibus];* **[et]c[etera]** is formed with tironian note, **c**, and mark of suspension.

VIII WILL 1506/7
***

In mongrel hand with splayed characteristics; on paper: page from probate register; Borthwick Institute of Historical Research, York, Prob Reg 6, page 185r - 186r.

In his will of 1507 Alderman John Stockdale, a York merchant, made arrangements for his burial in the Lady choir of St Michael-le-Belfrey, leaving money for masses to be sung for his soul. He willed money for the poor and for his children (legitimate and illegitimate).

1. In dei Nomi[n]e Amen the xxv day of Februarie the yere of our lord god M[il]l[esimo] Q[uingentesimo] vj th I
2. Iohn Stokdale of york Ald[er]man & Marchaunt in hole mynd & right witt mak[es] and
3. ordans my testame[n]t and last will in man[er] and forme

A will of 1507 from a York probate register.

folowyng Fyrst I gyff and

4. bequeth my saul vnto Almight god our lady saint marie & to all ye holy company

5. of hevyn and my body to be buried in saint Michaell kirk of Belfrey befor our

6. lady aut[er] in ye lady qwere so [tha]t ye preist when he doth masse than may stand apon

7. the end of the thurgh It[e]m I bequeth to be spentt aboutt me ye day of my buriall

8. in wax to p[re]st[es] & pore folk[es] v li[bras] It[e]m I bequeth to a p[re]st' to syng for my saule at ye

9. same alt[er] by iijth yerez next aft[er] my deceasse xiij li[bras] It[e]m I will and bequeth [tha]t Isabell

10. diconson my dought[er] haue her child[es] porc[i]on so [tha]t xx li[bre] which she had tofore be

11. Rekyned & acompt in ye same porc[i]on It[e]m I bequeth to Iohn Stokdale my bastard

12. son[n]e at kirkstall x marc[es] And to a bastard dought[er] of myn at hessyll w[i]t[h] a cosyn of

13. myn o[ther] x marc[es] It[e]m to ye wife [tha]t kepith her xxvj s[olidos] viij d[enarios]   It[e]m I bequeth to the

14. p[er]son of sant michaell kirk belfray for my forgotten tithes

xiij s[olidos] iiij d[enarios] And for my mor
15. tuarie my best garment ...

The scribe draws distinctive marks, interpreted as flourishes rather than abbreviation signs, notably through **ll** (**all**, line 4), over **th** (**bequeth**, line 7), and attached to terminal **n** (**hevyn**, line 5).

Line 1: **In dei Nomi[n]e** 'in the name of god'; Latin **Ml Q** rather than Roman numeral *M D* for 1500; **vj th**, 'sixth'.

line 4: **almight**, a normal form of 'almighty'.

line 6: **aut[er]**, 'altar'; **qwere**, 'choir'.

line 7: **thurgh**, 'through-stone, grave slab'; Stokdale, an influential citizen, commanded a prime site for his grave.

line 8: **v li[bras]**, '5 pounds, £5'; also (line 9) **xiij li[bras]**, '£13' and (line 10) **xx li[bre]**, '£20'; the **es** sign after the second **prest** is a clerical error, a singular was intended.

lines 12, 13: **x marc[es]**, '10 marks' = £6 13s 4d.

line 13: **xxvj s[olidos] viij d[enarios]**, '26s (shillings) 8d (pennies)', also (line 14) **xiij s[olidos] iiij d[enarios]**, '13s 4d' = 1 mark'.

line 14: **p[er]son**, fifteenth-century spelling and pronunciation of 'parson'.

lines 14-15 **mortuarie**, a customary perquisite to the parish priest.

In mongrel hand; paper indenture; National Library of Wales, Aberystwyth, Coed Coch 573.

The Coed Coch collection of documents is held at the National Library of Wales, the most important archive and research centre in the principality. This arbitration award of 1510 (number 573 in the collection) is in the Caernarfonshire section of the deeds, though the only location mentioned in the manuscript is the field-name *Ywern Vawr*.

Arbitration was a normal means of settling disputes. The arbitrator trod a difficult path through the sensitivities of parties who had, perhaps, nurtured resentments for years – or for generations. A skilled arbitrator, part psychologist, part diplomat, was well respected and equally well rewarded.

In this arbitration (an example of a Welsh legal document written in the Welsh language) the arbitrator Gruffydd ap Meredydd ap Dafydd attempts to settle a family squabble. He frames a resolution in which Rhys gives to Evan and Angharad, jointly, enjoyment of the produce of Big Meadow in lieu of cash for a debt owed by Isabel, who is (probably) a sister of Angharad. The nature of the relationship in which Rhys accepts responsibility for Isabel's obligations is not specified.

The names of the parties to the agreement show an interesting

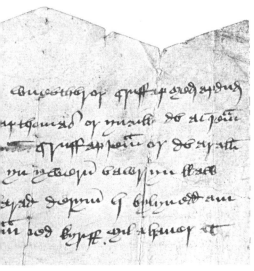

An arbitration award in Welsh made in 1510 in Caernarfonshire.

145

mixture of native Welsh names (Llywelyn, Meredydd) and Christian-introduced names (Jenkin – 'little John', David). The characters are identified not by surnames but by patronymics rehearsing small genealogies. Patronymics were formed with *ap*, 'son of', and *verch*, 'daughter of'. These patronymics began to fall from use during the sixteenth century, replaced by surnames – some with an (English) possessive s (as in Griffiths), others corrupted from patronymics (such as Bevan, from *ap* Evan*)*.

The arbitrator's decision was written out twice on a single sheet of paper. The two identical texts were separated by cutting the sheet in two. The cut was an irregular zigzag so that each half of the sheet had indentations corresponding to the other half along one edge (at the top in this case). The parties were each handed one half. In case of dispute in the future both texts had to be brought to the arbitrator or exhibited in court. If the indentations matched, it could be presumed that the documents had not been tampered with (that is forged). This type of written agreement is usually known as an **indenture** from the distinctive manner of cutting. A very common use was for apprenticeship agreements where one half was retained by the master and the other by the parents of the child who was apprenticed. Of course, three (or more) parties could be bound by a single agreement. For such occasions **indentures tripartite** (or **quadripartite**) were drawn up. In course of time indented cutting was deemed old-fashioned and unnecessary and was dispensed with. The word 'indenture', though, remained in use to describe all kinds of agreements and covenants.

1. bidybys ibawb ysydd ac addel rrac llaw wnevthvr or gruff ap Med' ap dud'
2. gylyvaredd rwnc Res ap Iankyn ap ll' ap thomas or ynaill dv ac Ieuan
3. ap Res ap ll' *or dv* ac yncharad V[erch] ap *Ieuan* gruff ap Ieuan or dv arall
4. abod yn amod ir Res adv gwair ysydd yn ywern vawr yn llaw
5. Iohn ap gruff ap belyn i Ieuan ac i yncharad derym vj bylynedd am
6. ddyledion oedd ar Isabel V[erch] gruff ap Ieuan oed kyrst Mil a haner ac
7. X *XI* bylynedd

Modern Welsh

Bydded yn hysbys i bawb sydd yn dyfod rhag blaen o wneuthuriad Gruffydd fab Meredydd fab Dafydd gymrodedd rhwng Rhys fab Siencyn fab Llywelyn fab Tomos ar y naill ochr ac Ieuan fab Rhys

fab Llywelyn ac Angharad ferch Gruffydd ap Ieuan o'r ochr arall,
ar yr amod i Rhys ollwng y gwair sydd yn y cae mawr yn law Ioan
fab Gruffydd fab Belyn i Ieuan ac Angharad am dymor o chwe
blynedd am ddyledion Isabel ferch Gruffydd fab Ieuan ym
mlwyddyn un fil pum cant a deg oed Crist

Line 1: **llaw**, a calligraphic flourish is added through **ll** as also in
arall (line 3) and **llaw** (line 4); a similar flourish serves an
abbreviative purpose in **ll[ywelyn]** (lines 2 and 3); **Med'** ... **dud'**,
terminal **d** finished with a downward flourish, arguably a mark of
abbreviation – presumably 'Meredith' and 'David'.

Line 3: **or dv** deleted; **V[erch]**, 'daughter of' – a common
abbreviation (also line 6); **ap** written in error but not deleted;
Ieuan written in error and deleted as the clerk too becomes confused by strings of patronymics.

Line 4: **ywern vawr**, literally 'meadow big' but translated as a
formal field-name rather than an informal description.

Modern English

Be it known to all who come henceforth of the making by
Griffith son of Meredith son of David of a compromise be-
tween Rhys son of Jenkin son of Llewelyn son of Thomas on
the one part and Evan son of Rhys son of Llewelyn and
Angharad daughter of Griffith son of Evan on the other part on
condition that Rhys relinquishes the hay which is in Big
Meadow in the hand of John son of Griffith son of Belyn to
Evan and to Angharad for the term of six years for the debts of
Isabel daughter of Griffith son of Evan. In the age of Christ one
thousand five hundred and ten years.

X BURGH COURT BOOK 1552
****

In secretary hand; on paper; page 349 of a bound volume; Moray
District Record Office, ZBE1 B2/1.

The lands of the town of Elgin were cultivated in the usual
medieval manner, with extensive common fields divided into strips
allocated among the burgesses and other tenants. Cattle were
pastured on moorland beyond the arable furlongs, and were also
grazed on stubble and fallow strips. This cooperative system was
regulated by custom and statute. The clerk of the burgh court, with
consent of the whole community, framed suitably pithy but precise
bylaws to protect the standing corn (oats and barley were the
Scottish staples) from cattle straying across the unenclosed landscape. The rules were enforced by the burgh court which had at its
disposal a scale of penalites including fines in cash and kind.

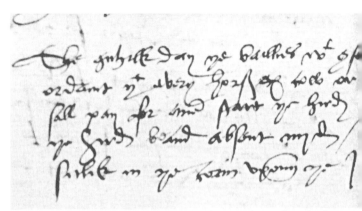

Bylaws to protect standing corn from cattle incursion, written in the burgh court book of Elgin, 1552

1. The quhilk day ye baillies w[i]t[h] [con]sent of ye haill ny[ch]tbo[u]r[is] p[rese]nt hes statut and
2. ordanit yt every horss ox cow or stirk yt beis fundin in ye corin heruest
3. sall pay for ane start ye hird being p[rese]nt sall pay ilk best Id and
4. ye hird beand absent iiijd/ and for ilk best yt beis fundin
5. siclik in ye corin vpoun ye I f[i]r[lot] vittuall

Line1: **The quhilk day** means 'the which day; the same day'. Each entry begins with this formula, referring the reader back to the heading 'burrowe court ... haldin ... ye ix day Maii ye zeir of god Imvc lij zer[is]'; **baillies** are the senior magistrates of the burgh; **haill ny [ch]tbo[u]r[is]** means 'whole (all) neighbours'; in **statut**, arguably the flourish on terminal **t** stands for **e** – 'statute and ordanit' was the common formula – but see also terminal flourish on **heruest** (line 2).

Line 2: **stirk** is a young bullock or heifer; **beis fundin** means 'be found'; **corin heruest** is 'corn harvest'.

Line 3: **start** means an incursion of grazing beasts which have leapt over a boundary on to a neighbouring pasture or crop – legalistically, 'start and o'erloup'; **hird**, the herders responsible for watching over grazing sheep and cattle were generally children, remembered in the popular rhyme *Little boy blue come blow up your horn;* **sall pay**, is a deleted dittograph; **ilk best**, 'every beast'.

Line 5: **siclik** means 'suchlike, similarly'; **vpoun**, 'upon', ends with a typical flourish; **I f[i]r[lot] vittuall** is ¼ boll (a measure of capacity) of grain – rents, fines, tithes, taxes and dues were customarily calculated and paid in victual.

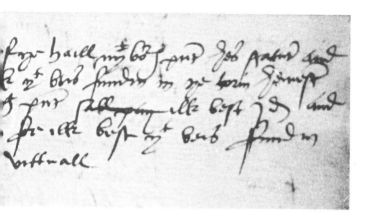

XI PARISH REGISTER 1588
***

In secretary hand with italic elements; on paper: one page in a
bound volume of the parish register of St Oswald, Durham; Durham Record Office, EP/Du.SO116.

This register of christenings is interrupted in 1588 (the year of
the Armada) for the announcement of a muster of local defence
forces on Spennymoor (north-east of Bishop Auckland)

1. Iohn' grene chrystened the xxviij of Iulye
2. Robert selby chrystened ye xjth day of august
3. Vpon munday beinge the xijth day of august, a[nn]o
   p[re]dicto, the Right' honorable earle of
4. hu[n]tington, lord presydent vnder o[u]r most gracyous
   sufferayne lady quene
5. elyzbethe, caused a generall muster to be vpon spenymore,
   of all p[er]sons w[i]t[h]in
6. thage of xvj and lx yeires, onely w[i]t[h]in the bysshopryke,
   & no farther,where
7. weare assembled on spenymore ye same day to ye full
   nu[m]ber of xl thowsa[n]de
8. me[n], redy to s[er]ve hyr magesty when the shuld be called,
   whome god
9. pres[er]ve longe to rayne ou[er] vs, a mother in Israell,
   Ame[n]
10. myles Rutt[e]r chrystend ye xxiiij of auguste
11. Francys martyn, christened ye xxv of auguste

Line 1: the scribal flourish through the ascender of **h** in **Iohn**
(also in **Right**, line 3) does not seem to represent an abbreviation.

Line 3: **Right' honorable** shows marked humanistic influence.

Lines 3, 4: **earle of Hu[n]tington**: Henry Hastings, third earl of Huntingdon, president of the Council of the North.

Line 9: Judges 5:7, 'The rulers ceased in Israel ... I Deborah arose ... a mother in Israel.'

XII ACCOUNTS 1598
***

In formal secretary hand, partly current; on paper: part of a page from a volume bound in a parchment leaf from a medieval book; Moray District Record Office, Forres, ZBE1 C60/1.

This account of the common good moneys of the burgh of Elgin was made on 2nd February 1597/8 in Thomas Hay's house in the presence of four bailies and four persons of counsel, for the terms of Whitsunday (15th May) and Martinmas (11th November) 1597. The accounts comprise *oneratio*, 'charge, cash received', and *exoneratio*, 'discharge, cash disbursed'.

1. Exoneratio
2. The Comptar viz' Androw edie discharges him of fourtie schilling[is]
3. debursit be him at ye townis co[m]mand for viueris to ye wyffis yat

A page, mainly of christenings, from the parish register of the church of St Oswald, Durham, 1588.

4. war wardit in ye stepill for witches in sy[m]mer Last bypast/ Item of
5. tue[n]tie schillingis for ane stane of tallown gevin to Robert lesly
6. to rewll ye knok w[i]t[h] co[n]form to ye townis p[r]ecept[is] & his acquittance
7. producit [thair]vpon /Item of thre lib' gevin be Androw Edie to ye
8. townis corrio[u]r[is] for wynnyng of certane hewin wark to ye tolbuith
9. co[n]forme to ye townis p[r]ecept[is] direct[it] [thair] vpon Item be Robert
10. kaith of tuentie schillingis for ane stane of tallown gevin
11. to Robert Lesly to ye kirk[is] cathekesing /Item of thre lib'
12. gevin to ye said[is] corryo[u]r[is] at ye townis co[m]mand and precept[is] /Item
13. of v[ther] tuentie schillingis gevin Indifferentlie to ye said[is] Robert
14. kaith & androw Edie for ane v[ther] stane of tallown to ye

Line 2: **Androw edie** (and **Robert kaith**, lines 9-10) were tacksmen of the town's customs – farmers and collectors of local tolls and taxes.

Line 3: **viueris**, 'victuals'; **wyffis**, 'wives, women'.

Accounts written in 1597/8.

Line 4: **wardit**, 'guarded, incarcerated'; **stepill**, 'steeple (of the tolbooth)'; /, the writer's characteristic punctuation mark.

Line 5: **Robert lesly**, reader and kirk session clerk of Elgin, responsible for catechising (line 11).

Line 6: **rewll**, 'oil'; **knok**, 'clock'.

Line 7: **[thair]vpon** extended in accordance with the writer's usual spelling; **n** finished with a calligraphic flourish; **thre lib'**, '£3'.

Line 8: **corrio[u]r[is],** 'quarriers'; **tolbuith**, 'tolbooth', the burgh's administrative headquarters, courthouse and gaol (see note to line 4).

XIII CALLIGRAPHIC SAMPLER 1610

a) ** In Gothic book hand and engrossing secretary hand; b) * in cursive humanistic hand; paper booklet; National Library of Scotland, Edinburgh, MS. 2197.

Professional calligraphers compiled samplers to demonstrate their own versatility and penmanship, and as an advertisement to attract students. Writing-masters proliferated during the sixteenth century, promoting the practice of fine writing in an age increasingly dominated by the printer's unlovely type and the scribbler's slovenly scrawl. The writing-master's sampler employed suitable aphorisms plucked promiscuously from religious, literary and historical works. For the writing-master the medium (the paper, ink and penmanship), rather than the content, was the message.

Hester Langlois (usually known as Esther Inglis) was a French protestant refugee. She was born in 1571 and married Bartholomew Kello, a Presbyterian minister in Edinburgh, in 1596. King James VI recognised in Esther Inglis 'the maist exquisit & perfyte wreater within this Realme'. The crown granted her the privilege of producing passports, testimonials, missives and other government documents, because 'it is verie requisit that al sik wreatingis be put in cumlie and decent maner of lettir and forme'. Convention required that the commission be addressed to Esther's husband!

Esther undertook private calligraphic commissions for the gentry and nobility of England and Scotland. One of her copies of the Psalms was inscribed 'A tres hant tres excellent et vertueux Prince, HENRY' (eldest son of James VI). She died in 1624 leaving her husband with several children and debts amounting to £156 Scots.

The calligraphic sampler demonstrates a variety of writing styles current in the early seventeenth century. The book was compiled from manuscripts (and texts) which crossed Esther's desk in the course of her daily copying and teaching work. The two pages chosen illustrate four hands of which she was master: firstly, a book hand (black letter, Gothic) of a type still used today where a medieval ambience is required – for example in heraldry and in church (a, line 1); secondly, the secretary hand which, when developed into 'court hand', continued into the nineteenth century to enhance the mystique of the civil service and the law (a, lines 2-6); thirdly, a sloped humanistic hand recognisable today in the printer's italic (b, lines 1-6); fourthly, flourishing capitals, ancestors of the copybook copperplate (b, lines 7-8).

(a)
1. God gaue to
2. mann a tounge to augmennt and maintaine the
3. gouermennte of manns life the maintenaunce thereof
4. Ioineth mann to mann in amitie: for all menn are of
5. the grounde: and Adam was created out of the yearth

Two pages from a calligraphic sampler of 1610 written by Hester Langlois (Inglis), the leading Scottish calligrapher of her day.

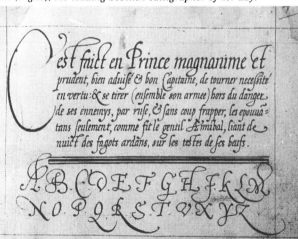

6.   but the Lorde hath deuided them by greate knowledge

(b)
1.   Cest faict en Prince magnanime et
2.   prudent, bien aduisé & bon Capitaine, de tourner necessité
3.   en vertu: & se tirer (ensemble son armee) hors du danger
4.   de ses ennemys, par ruse, & sans coup frapper, les epouua[n]
5.   tans seulement, comme fit le gentil Annibal, liant de
6.   nuict des fagots ardans, sur les testes de ses beufs.
7.   A B C D E F G H I K L M
8.   N O P Q R S T V X Y Z

(b)
It is necessary in a magnanimous and prudent prince, well-advised and a good commander, to turn necessity into virtue: and to extricate himself (together with his army) from the threat of his enemies, by guile, and without striking a blow, only terrifying them, as did the noble Hannibal, binding burning faggots by night on the heads of his oxen.

(a)
Line 1: **God**, initial **G** is formed by the foliage which frames the spear-carrying gentleman and unicorn – all demonstrations of the writer's skill.

Line 2: **n** and **u** are indistinguishable except in context; **n** is usually doubled; **tounge** is an acceptable seventeenth-century spelling, as is **maintenaunce** (line 3) which may reflect also Esther's French parentage and, presumably, her accent.

(b)
Line 1: **Cest**, the calligraphic flourish attached to the head of a large initial *C* is not an apostrophe – see **Capitaine** (line 2) and the alphabet (line 7).

Lines 5, 6: Hannibal of Carthage put a Roman army to flight by means of stampeding cattle during the Campanian campaign of the Punic wars in 217-6 BC.

Lines 7-8: early seventeenth-century usage did not employ distinct letter-forms for *I J* and or *U V W*; these forms were developed later in the century and not fully established until the eighteenth century.

XIV INVENTORY 1665
***

In late engrossing secretary hand, chiefly non-current, reflecting mongrel antecedents; on paper: single leaf; National Library of Wales, probate records, B1665 100 I/G.

The Woosnam family, originally (and named) from Wolstenholme, Lancashire, settled in central Wales in the seventeenth century. This inventory appraises, for probate purposes, the effects of a middling Montgomeryshire husbandman. Administration was granted in the court of the Bishop of Bangor in October 1665.

1. Ane Inventarie taken of all the good[es] Cattelse
2. and Chattel[es] moueabl and vnmoveabl of nicholas
3. wosenam of the p[ar]ish of llandinam and dioc[es]e of
4. bangor decessed the last day of august 1665
5. valued and prised by william wosenam
6. Robert wosenam and moraig prichard
7. Imprimis Kine oxen bulox and calefe
8. with two marese valued to – 20 li'
9. Ite[m] shipe and one swine valued to – 4 li'
10. Ite[m] Reie wot[es] and haye valued to – 6 li'
11. Ite[m] all Implement[es] of husbandrey to – j li'
12. Ite[m] all howsall stufe Brase phewter
13. beding[es] and bedstid[es]
14. with all bedclothese whatsoever to – 5 li'
15. Ite[m] his wearinge aparel to – j li'
16. Ite[m] his workinge tooles to – j li'
17. Somtoto thirty eight pownd[es]
18. valued and prised by william
19. wosenam Robert wosenam and
20. Morig prichard

Line 1: **good[es]**, property or possessions, later usually restricted to movables; **Cattelse**, from medieval Latin *capitale*, 'capital, sum of money', hence stock-in-trade.

Line 2: **Chattel[es]** from legal Anglo-Norman *chatel*, 'goods', hence any article of property other than real estate or freehold; **moueabl**, 'movable', hence personal rather than real property, as distinct from **vnmoveabl**, 'immovable' land, houses, etc.

Line 7: **calefe**, 'calf'.

Line 8: **marese**, 'mares'.

Line 9: **shipe**, 'sheep'.

Line 10: **Reie**, 'rye'; **wot[es]**, 'oats'.

Line 12: **howsall**, 'household'; **phewter**, 'pewter'.

Line 13: **bedstide**, 'bedstead'.

Line 17: **Somtoto**, 'sum total' from Latin *summa totalis*.

Line 20: **Morig prichard** signs her own name in humanistic hand with a tentative calligraphic flourish through **d**, though she has difficulty with **g**.

An inventory of the effects of Nicholas Woosnam who died in 1665.

XV MEMOIRS 1690
***

In the current mixed (secretary/humanistic) hand of a Scottish graduate; on paper: single page of a 350-page volume; Moray District Libraries, Elgin, DBL 79/1, page 228, presently listed as missing.

James Allan (1670-1740), a graduate of Aberdeen University and an individualistic preacher, compiled this memoir of his peripatetic ministry in Moray – with excursions to Aberdeen, Sutherland and (as here) to Edinburgh during 1689-91. The memoirs comprised some 350 closely written pages recording Allan's travels, opinions and the spiritual state of the nation – 'even as the Lord also has a book of remembrance'. Allan's book was intended for a wide readership and the manuscript probably enjoyed extensive circulation before reaching Paisley by way of Culross in Fife. The page reproduced concerns Allan's impending marriage, suggested by the famous Presbyterian preacher James Fraser of Brea (**Bray**, line 24) as a specific against Allan's 'manifold temptations'.

James Allan emerges through his own account as an uncompromising firebrand preacher, idolised by his female followers, vilified for his beliefs and continually at odds with the establishment. He was a writer of no little accomplishment. In the memoirs he is self-cast in the role of a prophet crying out against the sins of his people and constantly afflicted with headaches, toothaches, constipation, flatulence and an urgent adolescent sexuality.

James Allan's writing is distinctly English, though doubtless his secular speech and his sermons and lectures would have been broad Aberdeenshire 'doric' – a Scots dialect difficult for foreigners to understand even today. In the past, as now, people adopted different 'voices' for writing and for speech.

Allan's spelling is notably consistent even though there was no dictionary for him to refer to. (The earliest English dictionaries are those compiled by Nathaniel Bailey in 1721-6 and Samuel Johnson in 1755.) He prefers a double letter where modern usage prefers just one, as in **temporall** (line 19) and a single letter where we now prefer a double, as in **litle** (line 14). He uses **ie** rather than *y* at the end of words such as **seasoneablie** (line 3). The letter *e* is inserted where modern usage dispenses with it, as in **countenanceing** (line 16), and dropped where now required, as in **cam** (line 4) and **wrot** (line 11). All of this was normal English usage at the time.

228

1. kindlie intertained & M[arch] 31 got from him, after
2. some reluctancie & refuseing of it, 2 dollars which
3. cam very seasoneablie for my money was near
4. spent, returned to ye ferrie Capt[ain] Ro[ber]tsone being
5. with me, & lect[ured] [whe]r I left off. Ap[ril] 1. Cam in with
6. B.S. & M.S. in order to be marryed, haveing been
7. now thrice proclaimed: for we wer twice procl[aimed] in
8. one day, many things calling me to make haste
9. to return, haveing got more then one letter from
10. Echt earnestly intreating & obtesting my return
11. to that, I wrot to him this day shewing my present

kindlie intertained & M. 31 got from sim, after
some voluntarie & refusing of it, 2 dollars which
came very seasonable for my money was near
spent, returned to ye ferrie Capt Rossow came
with me, & left: q' I left off. Ap: 1. Came in with
B. J. & M. J. in order to be marryed, sabeing been
now twice proclaimed: for we wer twice procl: in
one day, many things calling me to make haste
to return, sabeing got more then one letter from
Echt earnestly introdating & obtesting my return
to haf, I wrot to sim his day schewing my present
purpose of marr: & of returning how soon wer possible,
also to my father. stayed in my ordinarie exercises etc.
Apr: 2. had some little trouble of body & was seeking
ye deliverance of it which I got in some measure
Ap: 3 found ye Lord greatly countenancing me in
every thing, many promises wer made very likely
& sweet to me, all I got befor confirmed & many
more, promises both of spirituall & temporall
things. In every thing I saw the Lord as a tender
hearted father, whereby my soul was much comforted
especially in that I saw I was not deluded, deluded
nor acted by my own spirit in ye matter I was
going about. O god pray to promise to remov trial
mortl

12. purpose of marr[iag] & of returning how soon wer possible,
13. also to my father. stayed in my ordinarie q[ua]rters & lect[ured].
14. Apr[il] 2. had some litle trouble of body & was seeking
15. ye removeall of it which I got in some measure, lectured
16. Ap[ril] 3 found the Lord greatly countenanceing me in
17. every thing, many promises wer made very lively
18. & sweet to me, all I got befor confirmed & much
19. more, promises both of spirituall & temporall
20. things. In every thing I saw the Lord as a tender
21. hearted father, wherby my soul was much comforted
22. especially in that I saw I was not deluded, deceived
23. nor acted by my own spirit in ye matter I was
24. going about. I got Bray to promise to come that night

Line 4: **ye ferrie** is Queensferry on the Forth.

Line 5: **Ap[ril] 1** is in italic script used by Allan for date, headings and biblical quotations. Note especially the form of p as contrasted with single-stroke secretary **p** in **spent** (line 4).

Line 6: the initials **M.S.** supply the only clue to the authorship of the memoirs; Edinburgh parish registers record the marriage of Margaret Steele and James Allan on 3rd April 1690; subsequently Margaret Steele was referred to only as 'my friend'; B.S. is Margaret's sister.

Line 9: **then**, obsolete form of 'than'.

Line 10: **Echt** refers to Arthur Forbes, laird of Echt (Allan's native parish) in Aberdeenshire.

Line 12: Scottish dialect **how soon wer possible** means 'as soon as possible'.

Line 13: though following a full stop **stayed** begins with a lower-case looped long s. Secretary long s is seen in **spent**, terminal s with ascender in **promises** (line 17). Small round-hand s occurs usually at the end of a word, as in **was** (line 3).

Line 21: though written small and at the edge of the page, every letter of **comforted** is carefully written; Allan writes two forms of **d**, one with a closed bow at the base, as in **dollars** (line 2), the other a splayed form with little or no bow as here, where the bow of the **e** occupies the space where the bow of the **d** would have been.

Line 22: only by looking at each cramped letter of **deceived**, written in full, can the word be read. **d** has a closed bow with looped ascender; secretary **e** (with high bow) and **c** (a single minim with attacking stroke – see **comforted**, line 21); secretary **e** with typical high bow hangs over a small (single minim) **i**; lower-case secretary **v** with ascender, resembling *b*, is more clearly seen in **haveing** (line 5); ed as in **comforted** (line 21).

... prayer ... ...
... The Coll for ÿ Poor was ... 2ˢ 0 4.
Janet Cromarty summoned to this diet, and thrice called
compeared not. James Cuming call'd, did compear, and
was earnestly pressed to confess his guilt, but stood to his
former denial. Being asked, if he was free to give his
oath in this matter; he answered he was. Janet Naugh-
tie summoned and call'd, compeared, and declared that, she
was witness to no unseemly carriage betwixt ÿ foresaid
James and Janet, And That all she knew was that
Thomas Stuart, Donald Calder, herself, the foresaid
James Cuming and Janet Cromarty being in one chamber, ÿ Lads were taking her by the hands, and sporting
together, but that there was no unseemly carriage betwixt any of them. She told moreover, that after the
Child was dead, Janet Cromarty had told her that the
Child was begotten in ÿ Common stable, when she was
sent out for fowls, and that she knew not who was the
person guilty with her, until afterward that she weep-
ing, he had said to her, Why do ye weep? If ye have a
bairn, I James Cuming will be the father of it? Then
John Sutherland and his servant Isabel Frazer being
called, told That all she said in their house, was That
seeing ÿ Child was dead, she car'd not a snuff for it,
whether he were sent for or not; Moreover the said Isabel informs that Janet Cromarty told her that ÿ Child
was begotten in ÿ nursery. Thereafter the said James
being call'd, The Nature of an oath, and the danger of
swearing falsly, was said before him, And by ÿ advice
of the Session, The Minister gave him ÿ form of an
oath, that he might have his thoughts thereof, and be-
ready to purge himself thereby next Sabbath.

*A record of a case before the kirk session of Kinneddar, Moray, on
23rd September 1710.*

XVI KIRK SESSION REGISTER 1710
*

In humanistic hand; on paper: page 88 of a bound volume; Scottish
Record Office CH2/384/2.

The kirk session (comprising minister, lay elders and deacons)
superintended the moral and spiritual life of the Scottish parish.
The session sat as a court; its minutes are, properly, registers of
discipline.

The kirk session of Kinneddar, Moray, became aware of a lapse
into fornication when, on 23rd September 1710, Janet Cromarty

desired baptism of her illegitimate child. She cited James Cuming (then in Aberdeen) as the father. The child died, but careful investigations into its paternity continued. It was established that the child was conceived at Gordonstoun (today, a famous public school) in the West-room, or in the nursery, or perhaps in the Common-stable. The case petered out as Cuming cleared his name by oath and Cromarty vanished 'no body knew whither'.

The careful humanistic script of John Watson, schoolmaster, precentor and session clerk is somewhat marred by the blackness of his ink, which bleeds through from the reverse of the page.

1. Janet Cromarty summoned to this diet, and thrice call'd,
2. compeared not. James Cuming call'd, did compear, and –
3. was earnestly pressed to confess his guilt, but stood to his
4. former denial. Being asked, if he was free to give his
5. oath in this matter, he answered, he was. Janet Naugh=
6. =tie summoned and call'd, compeared, and declared that she
7. was witness to no unseemly carriage betwixt ye foresaid
8. James and Janet, And That all she knew was that –
9. Thomas Stuart, Donald Calder, herself, the foresaid –
10. James Cuming and Janet Cromarty being in one cham=
11. ber, ye Lads were taking her by the hands, and sporting
12. together, but that there was no unseemly carriage be=
13. twixt any of them. She told moreover, that after the
14. Child was dead, Janet Cromarty had told her that the
15. Child was begotten in ye Common-stable, when she was
16. sent out for fowls, and that she knew not who was the
17. person guilty with her, untill afterward that she weep=
18. =ing, he had said to her, Why do ye weep? If ye have a –
19. bairn, I James Cuming will be the father of it? Then
20. John Sutherland and his servant Isabel Frazer being
21. called, told That all she said in their house, was That –
22. seeing ye Child was dead, she car'd not a snuff for it, –
23. whether he were sent for or not; Moreover the said Isa=
24. =bel informs that Janet Cromarty told her that ye Child
25. was begotten in ye nursery. Thereafter the said James
26. being call'd, The nature of an oath, and the danger of
27. swearing falsly was laid before him, And by ye advice
28. of the Session, The Minister gave him ye form of ane-
29. Oath that he might have his thoughts thereof, and be
30. ready to purge himself thereby next Sabbath.

Line 1: **this diet**, court session held on 5th November 1710; **call'd** is a typical eighteenth-century form.

Line 2: the curved line-filler **and–** (also lines 8, 9 etc) was inscribed to prevent fraudulent insertion and to achieve a pleasingly justified right-hand margin.

Line 3: **confess** employs long *s* and round *s*: **f** is clearly differentiated from long **s** by a tag to the right.

Lines 5-6: **Naugh=tie**, the double hyphen (also lines 10, 12, 17-18, 23-4) is characteristic of the time.

Line 9: **Stuart**, **S** is clearly differentiated from initial long **s** in **she** (line 8).

Line 18: **Why do ye weep**? has a curiously biblical timbre (see John 20: 13 and 15).

XVII SONG 1829
**

In cursive round hand; on paper; page from *First & Last of my Allbums, 1829*; J. & H. W. Leask, solicitors, Forres.

The songs of Archibald Duff Brands (1791-1869) of Forres, surgeon, town councillor, radical and poet, were set to music and performed to great acclaim at concerts in aid of local charities, such as the Forres free dispensary (established 1836) to which Brands gave of his medical talents *gratis*. In his *Song to Mary* Brands's romanticism is expressed in the lyrical ballad verse form, in the

The pen-drawn title-page of A.D. Brands's poetry album, 1829.

A song from 'First & Last of my All-bums' by Archibald Duff Brands, 1829.

charming rusticism of the 'humble cot' and in the self-conscious dialect of *ee, fan, awa, Frae, loo* (eye, when, away, from, love).

1. Song
2. Come again ye fleeting joys
3. ye Phantoms come to me
4. O come an bring wi marys form
5. Her bonnie blinkin ee

6. For fan a body's far awa
7. Frae body they loo dear
8. Tis neist to bliss to dream o them
9. An think ye see them near
10. To think ye haad, within your arms
11. the body ye loo best
12. An think ye kiss the rosy cheek
13. which leans upo' your breast
14. To think ye hear the faultring
15. wi downcast modest ee
16. Declare they'd scorn Ambitions Vows
17. For humble cot & thee

Line 4: **marys**, arguably a capital **M** intended; a similar problem is presented by initial **w** in **which** (line 13) and **wi** (line 15).

Line 7: **loo**, Scottish dialect 'love', though *loe* might be urged palaeographically on the evidence of upwardly flourished terminal **e; dear** terminal downward flourish (also **near**, line 9) presents palaeographical problems for **Vow(s)** in line 16.

Line 8: **bliss** (and **kiss**, line 12), note long **s**.

Line 16: **Ambitions Vows** seems more probably poetic, though **Ambitious vows** might be urged palaeographically.

XVIII REGISTER OF POOR 1883
*

In round hand; on paper; page 353 of a register; Grampian Regional Archives, ZPKe A5/102.

Alexander Johnston, Land Street, Keith, Banffshire, aged 59, a shoemaker, partially disabled by a chest complaint, was awarded three shillings (3/-) per week in poor relief by the parochial board (P.B.) of Keith, his native parish and thus his place of legal settlement. The inspector of poor noted that Johnston, a drug addict, made a little money from his trade and received a contribution from a grown-up son.

1. Johnston
2. Works at his trade and
3. makes 3/. or 4/. a Week
4. Birth and Residence
5. Wife, Mary Christie 49. born in Boyndie
6. Children
7. Elizabeth 10
8. John 8
9. Jane 5.
10. Alex[ande]r 25. R[ailwa]y Porter 18/. a week
11. pays rent for his father.

SPECIMEN TEXTS

12. Helen 27 married to R[ailwa]y Clerk
13. Mary 20. Has illegitimate child.
14. Annie 17. Has just had an
15. illegitimate child.
16. Pauper has acquired an
17. inveterate taste for Paragoric
18. or some other horrid opium stuff
19. which injures his health,
20. and leaves a smell in
21. the P.B. office for hours
22. after he has left.

Line 3: **3/. or 4/.**, unusual abbreviation, *3/- or 4/-* would be more

A page from the register of poor, Keith, Banffshire, 1883.

THE PARISH OF ___ *Keith*

Name	*Alexander*
Residence ...	*Land Street Keith*
Age ...	*59 Years*
Date of Minute of Parochial Board or Committee admitting Liability and authorizing Relief ...	*6th March 1883.*
Amount and Description of Relief authorized ...	*3/. a Week*
Country and Place of Birth, and, if in Scotland, Parish of Birth ...	*Scotland Keith*
Religious Denomination, whether Protestant or Roman Catholic ...	*Protestant*
Condition—If Adult, whether Married or Single, Widow or Widower ...	*Married*
If Child, whether Orphan, Deserted, or separated from Parent ...	
Trade or Occupation ...	*Shoemaker*
Wholly or Partially Disabled ...	*Partially*
Description of Disablement...	*Chest Complaint*
Wholly or Partially Destitute ...	*Partially*

Line 3: **3/. or 4/.**, unusual abbreviation, *3/-* or *4/-* would be more usual.

Line 5: **Mary Christie**, it was usual in Scotland for a married woman to retain her maiden name.

Line 17: **Paragoric**, paregoric elixir, a camphorated tincture of opium flavoured with aniseed and benzoic acid, readily purchased over the counter of the local chemist and druggist.

353

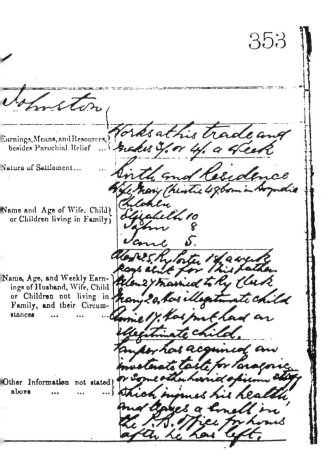

	Johnston
Earnings, Means, and Resources, besides Parochial Relief ...	Works at his trade and makes 3/. or 4/. a week
Nature of Settlement...	Birth and Residence
Name and Age of Wife, Child or Children living in Family	Wife Mary Christie 49 born in Boyndie Children Elizabeth 10 John 8 Jane 5.
Name, Age, and Weekly Earnings of Husband, Wife, Child or Children not living in Family, and their Circumstances ...	Alex 25, Ry Porter 18/ a week keeps dark for his father Helen 27 married to Ry Clerk Mary 20, has illegitimate child Annie 17, has just had an illegitimate child.
Other Information not stated above ...	Pauper has acquired an inveterate taste for Paragoric or some other horrid opium stuff which injures his health, and leaves a smell in the P.R. Office for hours after he has left.

15
Some useful textbooks

Backhouse, J. *The Lindisfarne Gospels*. Phaidon, 1981.

Backhouse, J. *Books of Hours*. British Library, 1985.

Barraclough, G. *Facsimiles of Early Cheshire Charters*. Record Society of Lancashire and Cheshire, 1957.

Bischoff, B. *Latin Palaeography: Antiquity and the Middle Ages*. Cambridge University Press, 1990.

Blackburn, B., and Holford-Strevens, L. *The Oxford Companion to the Year*. Oxford University Press, 1999.

Bowman, A.K. *The Roman Writing Tablets from Vindolanda*. British Museum, 1983.

Bowman, A.K. *Life and Letters on the Roman Frontier*. British Museum, 1994.

Boyle, L.E. *Medieval Latin Palaeography: a Bibliographical Introduction*. University of Toronto, 1984.

Brown, M.P. *A Guide to Western Historical Scripts from Antiquity to 1600*. British Library, 1990.

Budge, E.A.T.W. *An Egyptian Hieroglyphic Dictionary*. J. Murray, 1920.

Cameron, E. *An Introduction to Graphology*. Collins, 1989.

Chadwick, J. *Linear B and Related Scripts*. British Museum, 1986.

Claiborne, R. *The Birth of Writing*. Time Life International, Amsterdam, 1974.

Clanchy, M.T. *From Memory to Written Record: England 1066–1307*. Edward Arnold, 1979.

Cockerell, D. *Bookbinding and the Care of Books*. Pitman, 1901.

Danbury, E. *Palaeography for Historians*. Phillimore, Chichester, 1998.

Davies, W.V. *Egyptian Hieroglyphs*. British Museum, 1987.

Dawson, G.E., and Kennedy-Skipton, L. *Elizabethan Handwriting 1500–1650*. Faber, 1968.

De Hamel, C. *A History of Illuminated Manuscripts*. Phaidon, 1986.

Denholm-Young, N. *Handwriting in England and Wales*. University of Wales Press, Cardiff, 1954.

Diringer, D. *Writing*. Thames & Hudson, 1962.

Driver, G.R. *Semitic Writing from Pictograph to Alphabet*. Oxford University Press, third edition 1976.

Duncan, D.E. *The Calendar: the 5000 Year Struggle to Align the Clock and the Heavens and What Happened to the Missing Ten Days*. Fourth Estate, 1998.

Emmison, F.G. *How to Read Local Archives 1550–1700*. Historical Association, 1967.

Fairbank, A. *A Book of Scripts*. Penguin, revised edition 1968.

Friedrich, J. *Extinct Languages*. Dorset Press, 1989. (Translated from the German *Entzifferung Verschollener Schriften und Sprachen*, 1957.)

Gaur, A. *A History of Writing*. British Library, 1984.

Grieve, H.E.P. *Examples of English Handwriting. 1150–1750*. Essex Education Committee, Chelmsford, 1954.

Gullick, M. *Calligraphy*. Studio Editions, 1990.

Healey, J.F. *The Early Alphabet*. British Museum, 1990.

Hector, L.C. *The Handwriting of English Documents*. Edward Arnold, 1958.

Hector, L.C. *Palaeography and Forgery*. St Anthony's Press, 1959.

Hooker, J.T., et al. *Reading the Past*. British Museum, 1990.

Houston, S.D. *Maya Glyphs*. British Museum, 1989.

Humphreys, H.N., and Jones, O. *The Illuminated Books of the Middle Ages.* 1849; reprinted by Bracken Books,1989.

Ifrah, G. *The Universal History of Numbers.* Harvill Press, 1998. (Published in France as *Histoire Universelle des Chiffres,* 1994.)

Iredale, D. *Enjoying Archives.* Phillimore, Chichester,1985.

Jackson, D. *The Story of Writing.* Studio Vista, 1981.

Jenkinson, H. *The Later Court Hands in England.* Cambridge University Press, 1927.

Jennett, S. *The Making of Books.* Faber, 1973.

Johnson, C., and Jenkinson, H. *English Court Hand AD 1066 to 1500 Illustrated Chiefly from the Public Records.* Clarendon Press, Oxford, 1915.

Johnston, E. *Writing and Illuminating, and Lettering.* 1906; reprinted by A. & C. Black, 1977.

Knight, S. *Historical Scripts: a Handbook for Calligraphers.* Black, 1984.

Longhena, M. *Maya Script.* Abbeville Press, New York, 2000.

Mag Fhearaigh, C. *Ogham, an Irish Alphabet.* Ballagh Studios, Malin, County Donegal, 1993.

McLaughlin, E. *Reading Old Handwriting.* Federation of Family History Societies and Armstrong, Boon & Marriott, Birmingham, second revised edition, 1987.

Mell, G. *Writing Antiques.* Shire Publications, reprinted 1996.

Moorhouse, A.G. *Writing and the Alphabet.* Cobbett Press, 1946.

Morris, J. *A Latin Glossary for Family and Local Historians.* Federation of Family History Societies, Birmingham, 1989.

Munby, L. *Reading Tudor and Stuart Handwriting.* Phillimore, Chichester, 1988.

Naveh, J. *Early History of the Alphabet: an Introduction to West Semitic Epigraphy and Palaeography.* Magnes Press, Hebrew University of Jerusalem, 1982.

Newton, K.C. *Medieval Local Records: a Reading Aid.* Historical Association, 1971.

Nickell, J., Hamilton, C., and Van Outer, R.H. *Pen, Ink, and Evidence: a Study of Writing and Writing Materials for the Penman, Collector, and Document Detective.* Lyons Press, New York, 2000.

Noble, M., and Mehigan, J. *Collins Calligrapher's Companion.* Harper Collins, 1998.

O'Neill, T. *The Irish Hand.* Dolmen Press, Portlaoise, 1984.

Osley, A.S. (editor). *Calligraphy and Palaeography.* Faber, 1965.

Page, R.I. *Runes.* British Museum, 1987.

Parkes, M.B. *English Cursive Book Hands 1250–1500.* Oxford University Press, 1969.

Parkes, M.B. *Scribes, Scripts and Readers.* Hambledon, 1991.

Pope, M. *The Story of Decipherment, from Egyptian Hieroglyphs to Maya Script.* Thames & Hudson, 1999.

Reed, R. *Ancient Skins, Parchments and Leathers.* Seminar, 1972.

Richards, E.G. *Mapping Time: the Calendar and Its History.* Oxford University Press, 1998.

Robinson, P.R., and Zim, R. (editors). *Of the Making of Books, Medieval Manuscripts, Their Scribes and Readers.* Scolar Press, Aldershot, 1997.

Sassoon, R. *Handwriting of the Twentieth Century.* Routledge, 1999.

Simms, G.O. *Irish Illuminated Manuscripts.* Eason & Son, Dublin, 1985.

Simpson, G.G. *Scottish Handwriting 1150–1650.* Bratton, 1973.

Steinberg, S.H. *Five Hundred Years of Printing.* Faber, new edition 1959.

Walker, C.B.F. *Cuneiform.* British Museum, 1987.

Whalley, J.I. *The Art of Calligraphy.* Bloomsbury, 1980.

16
Glossary

Abacus: calculating apparatus, typically a frame of wires with sliding beads.

Algorism: Arabic or decimal system of numeration and calculation.

Alphabet: set of letters representing the basic sounds of a language.

Ampersand: word denoting the sign '&' meaning 'and'.

Annals: medieval narrative of events, typically year by year.

Antica: humanistic script (*litera antiqua*).

Arabic numerals: numerals (1-9 plus 0) derived from Arab script.

Archive: administrative document; popularly any ancient manuscript, or a place where such manuscripts are stored.

Ascender: part of an alphabet letter rising above the main line (as b, d, h).

Bastard hand: script blending book-hand and business-hand characteristics (1370-1525); the old name for mongrel hand.

Bestiary: medieval moralising encyclopedia of animals.

Binding: process of sewing together the leaves of a codex and securing the gatherings between protective covers; also the cover itself and associated cords, thread, etc.

Black letter: medieval (Gothic) book-hand script – especially as a printed typeface or romantic (Gothic) revival.

Board: stiff outer cover of a book.

Book: a written narrative; originally a wooden tablet for writing on.

Book hand: formal writing.

Book of Hours: medieval prayer book, usually illuminated, containing the eight services of 'the little office of the Virgin' to be recited at particular hours of the day.

Boustrophedon: writing in lines alternately left to right and right to left.

British: the Celtic language of the ancient Britons.

Buckram: stiff cotton fabric used in bookbinding; said to originate in Bukhara in Uzbekistan.

Business hand: handwriting of officials and businessmen.

Calendar: catalogue of archival documents arranged in date order; also a system showing the subdivisions of the year.

Calligraphy: handwriting as an art form.

Canon table: system for cross-referencing parallel gospel texts and stories.

Capital letter: large lettering for headings and initials derived from the Roman alphabet (upper case).

Carbon ink: suspension of lampblack or charcoal black.

Caret mark: sign / placed to show where omitted words should be inserted.

Carolingian script: reformed handwriting of the court of Charlemagne.

Cartouche: frame round a special word, such as the Pharaoh's name in Egyptian writing.

Cartulary: register containing copies of title deeds.

Case: protective covers for a bound book.

Celtic: Indo-European family of languages spoken before English in Britain and Ireland.

Chancery: legal and secretarial department of government.

Charter: formal document granting lands or privileges.

Charter hand: formal medieval administrator's script.

Chronicle: medieval record of events.

Codex: traditional bound book.

Colophon: tailpiece at end of old book, giving information now put on title-page.

Consonant: unvoiced sound made with the tongue, lips etc; also a letter indicating such a sound.

Contraction: abbreviation through reduction of a word to a few key letters.

Copperplate: calligraphic round hand.

Cornish: Celtic language of south-west Britain.

Court book: summary of proceedings in a court of justice especially a local court for a manor or borough.

Court hand: business and administrative script of the middle ages (not book hand); also specifically a script peculiar to a particular court or department of government.

Crossing: message written across a page, then across and at right angles to the first text to save paper and postage.

Cuneiform: wedge-shaped writing of the ancient Middle East.

Current: joined-up writing.

Cursive: rapidly written (usually sloped) script for everyday use.

Day: time taken for earth to rotate once.

Deed: a physical action; the written evidence of an action, especially if giving title to property.

Demotic: cursively written hieroglyphic script.

Departmental hands: scripts of government clerks (Pipe Office, Chancery, Exchequer, etc), sometimes called court hands.

Descender: part of an alphabet letter dropping as a tail below the line (as j, p, q, y).

Determinative: symbol in ancient writings indicating the type of word (animal, metal object, name of city, etc) which follows.

Die: engraved stamp for making an impression when sealing.
Diploma: official document.
Diplomacy: official communication between nations.
Diplomatic: critical analysis of old manuscripts.
Dittography: unintended repetition of a word or phrase.
Dorse: reverse side (of a parchment membrane).
Easter: spring festival named from pagan fertility goddess; Christian celebration of Jesus' resurrection.
Endorsement: writing on the back of a document.
Endpaper: paper folded into two leaves one of which is pasted inside the board of a book, the other remaining free as a blank leaf.
Engrossing: fair copying in large formal script for legal purposes.
Envelope: wrapper usually folded or glued for enclosing private papers. Ancient Mesopotamian wrappers were made of clay.
Erse: Irish (Gaelic) language.
Erse script: modern Irish writing in insular minuscule manner.
Exchequer: financial department of government.
File: bundle of papers strung together on a string or wire, from Latin *filum*, 'thread'; also any bundle of papers, especially if contained loosely in a cardboard cover or envelope.
Flyleaf: the blank pages at the front and back of a bound book.
Folio: sheet of paper folded to form two leaves.
Foolscap: a paper size 16¼ by 13 inches (sometimes 13 by 8 inches) (413 by 330 mm; sometimes 330 by 203 mm): the image of a fool or jester with cap-and-bells was used as a watermark.
Forgery: document falsification.
Fount: collection of type of the same size and typeface.
Free hand: medieval script for everyday use allowing certain leeway in letter-forms.
Futhork: runic alphabet of the Anglo-Saxons and Norsemen.
Gaelic: the form of Celtic language spoken in Scotland and Ireland.
Gathering: papers folded and stitched together as a booklet.
Gloss: word for word (often interlined) literal translation.
Glottal stop: sound made by opening and closing the windpipe as in Cockney pronunciation of butter (bu'er).
Gospel book: book containing one or more accounts of Jesus' life (Matthew, Mark, Luke and John).
Gothic: medieval style; also eighteenth-century revival of medieval style, often written with 'k' as Gothick.
Graffiti: informal writing, usually on walls.
Graphology: analysis of personality from handwriting.
Gregorian calendar: calendar devised for Pope Gregory XIII (New Style).

Guttural: sound made in the back of the throat, as ch in loch.

Hagiography: writings about a saint's life.

Half-uncial: script of early Christian Ireland.

Haplography: writing error arising when a letter, word or phrase is written once only when it should be written twice.

Hatchment: wooden board painted with the coat of arms of a deceased person; also known as achievements.

Heraldry: art and science of coats of arms.

Herbal: encyclopedia of useful plants.

Hieratic: formal hieroglyphs for writing in ink on papyrus.

Hieroglyphic: pictorial and symbolic script of ancient Egypt.

Homily: sermon.

Hour: unit of time defined by man.

Humanistic hand: reformed script of the Renaissance (fifteenth century onwards).

Ideograph: pictorial representation of an idea.

Illumination: decorative and colourful embellishment.

Indenture: type of document recording an agreement.

Indiction: calendar cycle of fifteen years.

Indo-European: related peoples and languages of India, Middle East and Europe.

Ink: writing fluid; the word derives from the Greek meaning 'burnt-in', alluding to the permanence of ancient inks.

Insular minuscule: spiky early medieval script of Britain and Ireland.

Iron-tannin ink: acidic medieval ink of rust-brown colour.

Italic: cursively sloped humanistic writing; also a sloped typeface.

Julian: calendar devised for Julius Caesar (known as Old Style dating).

Laid paper: paper with fine parallel and cross lines produced during manufacture and evident when held up to the light.

Latin: language of the Roman empire.

Leaf: a single thickness of paper or parchment forming two pages in a book.

Legend: the words or motto on a seal.

Letter book: bound volume of copy letters.

Letter patent: charter issued open for all to see, often addressed 'to all men'.

Ligature: tag joining letter to letter.

Lower case: printer's term for ordinary small lettering; literally the lower tray containing the small type.

Majuscule: letters of equal height, without ascenders and descenders (e.g. block capitals).

Manuscript: writing done by hand – not printed.

Manx: Celtic language of Isle of Man.

Matrix: the die or master from which seal impressions are taken.

Membrane: a skin or leaf of parchment.

Mesopotamia: territory watered by rivers Tigris and Euphrates.

Middle English: the language of England and Scotland 1100-1500.

Minim: a single vertical penstroke (as forming i, m, n, u, etc).

Minuscule: lettering with ascenders and descenders.

Minute: written record of a meeting.

Mixed hand: script mingling humanistic and secretary elements.

Mnemonic: a memory aid (such as a knot in a handkerchief or a form of words like 'Every good boy deserves favours' giving the notes of the musical stave E, G, B, D, F).

Modern English: English used since the late fifteenth century.

Mongrel hand: script blending book-hand and business-hand characteristics (1370-1525), also known as bastard hand.

Monogram: character formed of two or more letters, often a person's initials, interwoven.

Month: measurement of time relative to the moon's phases.

Morocco: fine, pebble-grained leather originating in Morocco and made from goat skins; favoured for bookbinding.

Muniment: title deed relating to landed property; popularly all kinds of archival records, especially private estate and family papers.

New style: the Gregorian calendar of 1582.

Norman French: language of France and England under Norman rule.

Norn: Norse language of Shetland.

Norse: Scandinavian (Denmark, Norway, Sweden).

Notae juris: shorthand symbols used in legal writings.

Notary Public: Scottish legal practitioner.

Obverse: front page of a leaf of parchment or paper.

Octavo: a paper size; also a book formed of pages folded three times to give eight leaves from one sheet.

Ogham: inscriptional writing of early Ireland.

Old English: the language of the Anglo-Saxons.

Old Irish: the Celtic language of Ireland.

Old style: the Julian calendar of 46 BC.

Page: one side of a leaf of parchment or paper.

Palaeography: the study of old handwriting.

Palimpsest: parchment which has been written on, scraped clean and reused.

Paper: writing material manufactured from linen rags, wood, pulp, etc.

Papyrus: writing material of the ancient world manufactured from Egyptian papyrus reed.

Paraph: calligraphic flourish, often added to a signature as an individuating feature and precaution against forgery.

Parchment: writing material manufactured from animal skin.

P-Celtic: the Celtic language of Britain including Wales.

Pen: implement for writing with ink, fashioned from a reed or a feather.

Pencil: graphite writing implement; also a fine paintbrush.

Pendant: hanging from, usually applied to a seal hanging from a document.

Penknife: scribe's knife for shaping quill pens and scratching out mistakes.

Phonogram: symbol representing a spoken sound.

Pictograph: pictorial representation of an object.

Picture: drawing of object, particularly to convey message.

Pipe Office: financial department of government dealing with county sheriffs.

Pipe roll: parchment roll recording financial accounts of county sheriffs.

Pounce: fine powder sprinkled on to wet ink to act as blotting paper.

Protocol book: Scottish lawyer's register of deeds and contracts.

Psalter: book of Psalms.

Punctum delens: ink dot indicating words or letters written in error to be ignored by the reader.

Q-Celtic: the Celtic language of Ireland and Scotland.

Quarto: a paper size formed by folding a traditional sheet twice, making four leaves.

Quill: central rib of a feather used as a pen.

Quipu: bundle of knotted cords used to convey messages in the Inca empire.

Record type: typeface devised for printed transcriptions of medieval writings.

Recto: front of a leaf; right-hand page of a book.

Regnal year: chronology based on years counted from the accession of a monarch.

Roll: sheets or membranes sewn, glued or strung together, then rolled up for storage; chiefly official documents.

Roman type: serifed typeface derived from humanistic script.

Romantic Revival: eighteenth-century revival of interest in medieval (Gothic) style.

Round hand: cursive current looped English script blending secretary and humanistic elements.

Rubric: letters, words or phrases highlighted in red.

Runic: writing of early medieval Germanic people.

Russia: type of leather.

Rustic capitals: condensed Roman book-hand lettering.

Sasine: Scottish title deed.

Schoolman: medieval university teacher, particularly of theology and philosophy.

Scots: dialect of Middle English used in Scotland.

Script: handwriting, especially a particular style of writing (business script, secretary script, etc.).

Scriptorium: writing and book-production department of a monastery.

Scrivener: professional copyist of documents.

Seal: impressed design (usually in wax) for authenticating documents.

Secretary hand: business script of the sixteenth century.

Semitic: Western Asiatic peoples (Palestinians, Arabs, Syrians, etc.).

Sennachie: Gaelic tribal elder, bard or seer.

Serif: cross-stroke at the head or foot of a vertical stroke of a letter.

Set hand: distinctive script of a government department.

Shorthand: system of speed writing using symbols and shortened words.

Sign manual: handwritten signature for authenticating a document.

Signature: manuscript authentication for a document using a person's own name.

Size: liquid manufactured from boiled-down hoof, horn or parchment used to give stiffness and 'rattle' to paper.

Solstice: midwinter and midsummer.

Spiky minuscule: handwriting of England and Ireland from the seventh to the eleventh century.

Splayed hand: mongrel script with letter-forms sprawling sideways.

Stele: upright stone column carved with inscriptions.

Stylus: pointed writing implement.

Substitution: abbreviation by using a symbol to stand for a word or part of a word.

Superscript: letter or symbol written above the main line of writing.

Suspension: abbreviation by using only initial letter(s) of words.

Syllable: two or more letters representing a spoken sound.

Symbol: mark conventionally denoting an object or idea.

Tally stick: notched stick for medieval accounts.

Textus: medieval (Gothic) book hand.

Thorn: runic letter for th.

Tironian note: shorthand symbol from the system supposedly invented around 40 BC by M. Tullius Tiro.

Title deed: written evidence for the ownership of property.

Tooling: ornamental embossed or stamped work on the binding of a book.

Transcription: copy of a text preserving the original appearance of the writing.

Translation: process of changing from one language or mode of speech to another.

Transliteration: copy of a text rendering ancient or foreign letter-forms and symbols in normal Roman type or modern conventional handwriting.

Triskele: characteristic curvilinear three-legged ornament employed in Celtic art.

Type: metal or wooden block with raised letter for use in printing.

Typeface: impression made by type on a page; the style of the typed 'writing'.

Uncial: 'inch high' book hand of early Christian Europe.

Upper case: printer's term for capital letters.

Vademecum: a handbook or textbook (from Latin words meaning 'go with me').

Vellum: parchment made from calf skin.

Versal: special large (usually coloured and decorated) initial letter.

Verso: the reverse side of a leaf; the left-hand page of a book.

Vowel: letter of the alphabet representing a basic voiced sound (a, e, i, o, u).

Wafer: adhesive disc used to stick down a folded document; often red paper stuck on surface of legal record.

Watermark: manufacturer's trade mark in paper.

Wax: beeswax for sealing documents.

Wen: runic letter for w.

Wove paper: paper with pattern of fine mesh visible when held up to the light.

Writing: means of communication using symbols to represent spoken sound.

Year: the time taken for the earth to circle the sun.

Year book: medieval report of law cases.

Year of grace: chronology of years counted from the birth of Jesus Christ (Anno Domini, 'In the year of the Lord', AD).

Yogh: letter representing guttural sounds in Anglo-Saxon and Middle English.

Index

INDEX

INDEX